et's
t on a
HOW

ide to Fun
ndraising for
Community
anization

& Colleen Schuerlein

Let's
Put on a
SHOW

A Guide to Fun
and Fundraising for
Your Community
Organization

Gail Brown & Colleen Schuerlein

Let
Put on
SHO

A Guide to
and Fundraisin
Your Commu
Organizatio

Gail Brown & Colleen S

To Coleen!
Love from one
ya ya to another.
Gail Brown

D1739201

ALLWORTH PRESS
NEW YORK

10 09 08 07 06   5 4 3 2 1

Published by Allworth Press
An imprint of Allworth Communications, Inc.
10 East 23rd Street, New York, NY 10010

Cover design by Derek Bacchus
Interior design by Joan O'Connor
Typography by Integra Software Services
Interior images courtesy of Cordelia Ransom

ISBN: 1-58115-442-9

Library of Congress Cataloging-in-Publication Data:

Brown, Gail, 1939–
   Let's put on a show: a guide to fun and fundraising for your community/Gail Brown and Colleen Schuerlein.
      p.   cm.
   Includes index.
1. Amateur theater–Production and direction.   2. Fund raising.   I. Schuerlein, Colleen.   II. Title.

   PN3156.B76 2006
   792.02'220232–dc22

                                                        2006006925

Printed in Canada

This book is lovingly dedicated
to the Orcas Island cast and crew who
shared their time, talent, and energy
by participating in the variety shows
we had the honor of co-producing.
You are Love Made Visible.

Contents

★ 1 GETTING STARTED ★

⭐ 2 GETTING READY ⭐

⭐ 3 ONSTAGE ⭐

⭐ APPENDIXES ⭐

Acknowledgments

A heartfelt thank you to the following people, who are truly an inspiration in our lives and without whom this book would not have been possible.

Thank you to the staff at Allworth Press and special gratitude to our editor, Nicole Potter-Talling, whose encouragement, support, and creative suggestions took our ideas to a whole new level.

To all the creative people who contributed their "Stories from the Stage," sharing theater experiences, wisdom, and insights. We applaud you.

A special thank you to Thelma McTavish, Abby Rueb, Frances Harvey, Marguerite Olson, Tim Ransom, Velma Doty, and Phyllis Carney for their contributions to the history of entertainment, fun, and fundraising on Orcas Island through the years.

To our dear friends, Cristy Bethel, Rick Brandeburg, Nancy Craddock, Dean Forseth, Karen Hanzlik, Jackie Henry, Rhoda Klune, Dorothy Manin, Claudia Moorad, Jackie Norris, Barbara Ramsey, Michael and Kristen Schuerlein, Charlotte Steinhorst, David and Mary Stockton, Wendy Williams, Mike Schifsky, Susan Wiley, and Paula Wirth for their continued belief and support in our life and our project.

We would like to give special thanks as well to our Orcas friends, Duff and Marilyn Andrews and George and Marcia Spees. Thanks for the memories.

To "The GGs," Colleen's Partners in Believing: Debbie Tallman, Rev. Faith Moran, and Rev. Mary Manin Morrissey. Thank you for sharing the journey with me. Your friendship is a blessing in my life.

To our wonderful children, Shannon Hudson, Michele Shane, and Nick Brown. We admire you for living your life's passion as teachers. Thank you for gracing us with your continued love and support. You, your spouses—John, Steve, and Caryn—as well as your children—Ian, Erik, Peyton, Ryan, Sylvie, and Mack—bless our lives with love that is beyond words.

To Colleen's brother, Bob Hasbrook, I am deeply grateful for your presence in my life.

To Colleen's mom, Lucile Hasbrook, whose guidance and love continue to be a bright light in both our lives.

Our deepest appreciation to Doug Brown who assisted us in gathering stories from people across the nation, and his invaluable advice and editing support. Thank you, Doug, for helping us bring this book to life.

—Gail Brown and Colleen Schuerlein

Preface

Fundraising is more important today than ever before. With government and public funding and grants being cut, many organizations, schools, churches, and community theater groups are left on their own to support their programs. We wrote this book to share our experiences in producing and directing variety shows on Orcas Island, a remote island in Washington State, to help raise money for a Community Center for the Arts.

Orcas has a rich history of people who love drama, music, and art. In the forties and fifties, variety shows were presented at the Grange Hall to raise money for the March of Dimes and other worthy causes. These fun-loving people joined together to entertain friends and neighbors while doing something to help others. June Schulberg, a wonderful pianist, along with Abby Rueb, Thelma McTavish, Sadie Gow, and other talented people, staged variety and scripted musicals during the sixties, seventies, and eighties to raise money for various causes, one of the most memorable being a production of *The Fantasticks*. (Many of the participants later joined us when we did our "Orcas Tonight" presentations.) During this same period of time, Earl Eastman and "The Magic Medicine Show" was a big attraction after the annual Fourth of July parade and at the Library Fair. Earl and his partner performed acrobatic acts and sold bottles of Eastman's Magic Elixir from their rustic wagon.

The Orcas Players produced their first of many plays in 1963. They opened with *Arsenic and Old Lace* and made enough money to present a scholarship to a graduating senior interested in the performing arts. This group spawned the idea of building a theater for local productions. Years later, a beloved high school English teacher took it to the next level and called a meeting for anyone interested in pursuing this dream.

When the two of us said, "Let's put on a show!" we were not the first, and certainly not the last, to do so. When you live on an island, you learn to entertain yourselves. Now that the Orcas Center for the Arts is built, it is booked solid year round with plays, musicals, children's programs, musical presentations, visiting symphonies, art displays, dances, banquets, theater classes, and visiting musicians and artists from the mainland.

—Gail Brown and Colleen Schuerlein

Introduction

This book is about what we did. We plan to pass on some of the things we did, and the lessons we learned, as well as stories from community and professional theaters around the country that have experienced similar situations, with the hope that we can teach, amuse, and inspire you.

In the seventies, our home, Orcas Island, was a small community of about 2,000 people in the San Juan Islands of Washington State. Orcas was a tight little place, mostly old farm families with a group of newcomers from Seattle and hippies from California all trying to fit in. It was a diverse but close-knit group of people who depended on one another for friendship and acceptance. When anyone had trouble of any kind, the whole island came together to help.

Colleen, mother of two daughters, started a recycling center, managed an island resort, counseled teenagers with problems, worked at the local pharmacy, and volunteered at the school. She is now an ordained minister in Portland, Oregon who facilitates and participates in secular and interfaith projects.

Gail was the fourth grade teacher at the local school, who believed in theater as an educational tool. Some of her students went on to professional careers in theater, film, and television. All her students remembered the parts they played in the fourth grade play. Music, art, and drama were an integral part of her teaching strategies, and most effective when used to teach the basic skills of reading and writing. Colleen and Gail spent much of their time raising money for island projects.

Margaret Exton initiated the idea for the Community Center for the Arts. One afternoon, others joined her in her living room to talk about how we could build a center, and, at the same time, provide a place for school kids to gather. All agreed it was a grand idea. Everyone worked hard. We had bake sales, car washes, dances—the usual things groups do when they have to raise money. However, it soon became obvious it was going to take lots of cakes, cars, and casino nights, plus some hefty grants and donations, to finally build a building. Although we knew our contributions wouldn't be nearly enough to fund the whole project, we wanted to do everything we could to contribute. We had big ideas, great people, and lots of energy, but we were short on fundraising power.

One night, the two of us were brainstorming fundraisers in keeping with the community's vision and all of a sudden, we said, "Hey, let's put on a show!" It seemed to be the perfect fit for a Center for the Arts as it would involve all the creative people in town, bring them together in a unique way, and be a lot of fun! We began taking notes, and soon we saw the whole show in our minds. We listed acts we would need so the show would appeal to everyone, young and old. Sha Na Na was big at the time, so we wrote that down. Dolly Parton, Barbra Streisand, Johnny Cash and June Carter Cash, and Jerry Lee Lewis were added. However, we didn't want a show with singers only. We wanted Variety! A juggling act? Soft shoe? Skits? How about Kermit the Frog and Big Bird for the little kids, a jitterbug number performed by teenagers and even some commercials for local businesses? We had plenty of material!

There were two problems. Since we had no Center, we had no place to stage a show, and since many newcomers had arrived on the island, we had no idea how many had the talent that would be needed to create the production we envisioned. Well, we could use the school, the drafty old Grange Hall, or the dining room in the abandoned Madrona Inn. We'd find something.

The entire brainstorming session took less than twenty-five-minutes and we were so excited, one of us said, "Who could be Sha Na Na? There must be some guys at the town hangout who can do it." We drove to the center of town, walked into the most popular place, looked around, and started pointing.

"Dave, Mike, Terry. You, you, and you. We're going to put on a show to raise money for the Center for the Arts and we need a Sha Na Na group."

"Hey, wait a minute! What? You're crazy! What're you talking about? I was kicked out of chorus in the seventh grade."

"We want you guys to be Sha Na Na."

"But we can't sing!"

"I couldn't pass chorus."

"I don't have the time."

"Oh, we think you can. Schifsky, we're using your barn. You guys meet us tomorrow night at 7:00 and we'll practice."

We marched out, and the next night at 7:00, they all showed up: a couple of construction workers, the water district guy, a loader from the lumberyard, a lineman for the county, and a contractor, all looking extremely skeptical and scared about the whole thing. We lined them up and shoved a dead "mike" at Dave Roseberry because we knew he could sing. Dave took the microphone, looked at the group and belted out "Here's my story, sad but true . . . " some of the guys chimed in with a weak doo-wah. Rosebud rolled right into "It's about a girl that I once knew . . . " and before they knew it, they were all rocking out "Runaround Sue" with no accompaniment. Colleen's nine-year-old daughter, Shannon, who had been quietly watching, jumped up and started dancing and choreographing their moves. Before 9:00, they were all having a great time, and amazed at themselves.

The next evening, the house band from the resort came to the barn and the leader, Larry Schacher said, "I can help any group of people sing. Bring these guys on!" Within minutes, the group was singing and six stars were born. Larry, already a long-time regional, professional "star," cranking on his sax, was scooting across the floor on his knees.

"Hey, we sound good!" They did, indeed, and proved to be one of the hits of the show. Just goes to prove that talent lives and waits to be awakened in the most unexpected places. From that point on, the show gained a life of its own. Our Dolly Parton revealed she had sung in the church choir. Gary Plummer, our Johnny Cash, knew three chords on the guitar and when he and Mary Ann, our June Carter Cash, sang "We got married in a fever . . . " from the song "Jackson," you would have sworn you were listening to the real artists. Word spread rapidly and suddenly everyone had a talent. We had skaters, magicians, and actors who wanted to be in skits and commercials for the local businesses. Within days, groups were practicing in kitchens, basements, and garages all over the island. The two of us were elated and somewhat surprised at how well the whole thing was coming together. We drove from group to group, critiquing, making suggestions for costumes, hair-styles, and backup music. It was like magic and before we knew it, we had ninety-two people of all ages involved.

The venue problem still remained. Both the Grange and the school gym were too small, but Rosario Resort Hotel, the tourist attraction on the island, had just completed a convention center that would hold 300 people, so we went to the owner, Gil Geiser, and told him our plans to help build a Center for the Arts. He generously donated the new convention center for our project. We now had to find local carpenters to build a stage and backdrops, electricians to install lights, locate sound equipment, and try to find a band.

Orcas Island Community Center for the Arts

Of course, "can-do" people emerged from all parts of the island, and we were certain we had angels on our shoulders guiding us. Within four months, we presented the first of many "Orcas Tonight" variety shows. We played to a standing-room-only crowd and the cash box was over-flowing. The friendships that were formed and the pride in reaching new levels of achievement made us know we were working together for a common cause. Each participant—from hairdressers to technical crew to headliners—knew they were doing service and participating in an opportunity to express their unique talents to the world (well, at least to the island).

The minute the final curtain fell, people were saying, "Let's have another show next year!" Our philosophy of inclusion rather than exclusion gave everyone an investment in the original show and allowed them to form bonds (many unexpected) that would never be broken. Besides, we had enjoyed ourselves and entertained our friends and neighbors.

☆ "Next Year" Is the Reason We Wrote This Book ☆

Our first show had been so effortless and completely successful, we expected the same thing to happen again. Apparently, that first year we had been operating on beginner's luck. The second year, dress rehearsal was a total disaster. People were late, some didn't show up at all, props were missing, microphones didn't work, and we were bombarded with a million questions for which we had no answers. One of the longtime, professional musicians sitting next to us at the back of the auditorium watching this unfold, turned and said, "If you two can pull this off by tomorrow night, it'll be a miracle." We looked at him, and then at one another, and said, "We may have to return the money from advance ticket sales." Then turned and said, "No, Doc, trust us. It's going to happen!"

There is an old saying that a bad dress rehearsal bodes a good performance, but this was disastrous. We had to get our acts together, or be prepared to return the money and let the stage go dark. At the end of rehearsal, we asked the cast and crew to come in two hours early the following night, and (since they knew exactly what we knew) everyone said, "We'll be here," and the two of us got to work. We had to fix the mess we were in.

We made lists of the things that had gone wrong. We made cue cards, signs directing people where to go and what to do, prepared a pep talk, had our do-it-all guy check all the equipment, and generally got our acts together in an organized fashion. (We could have used this book had it been written at the time!) Of course, the cast and crew responded. They showed up and everybody was ready to go. The sequence was perfect and the technical production was flawless. The show turned out to be not just a success, but a rousing success. People in the audience were clapping so hard during the finale their hands were red. Some were standing on chairs to applaud, and tears of laughter were rolling down their cheeks. We felt as though we had sent a love note to the community and they were sending the love back to those onstage.

We were novice directors who made a positive difference in our community. And you can, too. Whether you're working to buy computers for your school, send aid to disaster victims, build a new church, or simply buy uniforms for a Little League team, this book will help you. It will help organize, produce, and direct a fantastic variety show, make new friends, discover hidden artistic talent, and make a whole lot of cash—all while having the time of your life.

Today, the Orcas Island Community Center for the Arts is a multi-use building, constructed in typical Northwest style with wooden siding. It has a low profile set among Douglas firs and is beautifully landscaped. The signature element, as you drive onto the property is a huge metal sculpture of an Orca Whale, created by local metalsmith and artist Pete Welty. The building has a community kitchen, meeting rooms, and a hall with accordion dividers so two groups can be accommodated at the same time. This space is also used for rehearsals, choreographing, fundraising activities, and as a gathering place for refreshments during intermissions. The foyer is large and the walls are

Orca Whale in front of Orcas Island Community Center for the Arts

always adorned with the artworks of the many fine local artists. The theater seats 215, the backstage is fully outfitted and provides spaces for costume changes and large, complicated productions. Lighting and sound is up-to-date and capable of handling all theatrical challenges. The Center is in use daily as a venue for professional and amateur plays, symphonies, art shows, children's productions, concerts, and guest visits by famous performers.

When we go back to the island and see the completed Orcas Island Community Center for the Arts, we have a sense of pride in knowing we played a small part in making this dream come true. We feel grateful to all the people who said yes, and who helped to build the center, and to those who continue to fund and operate this special place. We want you, the reader, to share this sense of involvement in your cause and enjoy very minute of it.

—Gail Brown and Colleen Schuerlein

GETTING STARTED

....

CHAPTER 1

Let's
Put on
a Show

So you want to raise some money for a worthwhile project, and you think you'll put on a show to raise some funds. You are jut getting started, and you consider *Cabaret*, *Cats*, and maybe *All My Sons*. How can you go wrong with proven winners and great classics!? Well . . . have you considered a variety show? If you haven't, read on.

☆ Stories from the Stage ☆

This is the first of many stories you will come upon in this book, and this one is ours.

Way back in 1961, in Austin, Texas, Gail began teaching and was assigned a class of twenty-five fourth graders; Gail felt like she was in heaven. She began the year introducing basic skills, designing art projects, and getting to know the students. She noticed that different students learned in different ways, and many of her fourth graders still could not read. "Aha!" It hit her. They needed to learn to read with expression and comprehension. She recalled her own wonderful times onstage and thought, "Let's put on a show!"

Thanksgiving was approaching. She found a little booklet of plays for children and chose a short, scripted play about the first Thanksgiving, put it on the mimeograph machine and gave each child a faded, purple-inked script.

From the start, she knew every student had to be involved in some way, and although the script only called for eight parts, she expanded the script to include every child in the class. She quickly threw out the script, kept the idea, and asked the class to create parts so everybody could be onstage. She had less than a month to prepare, and since she had never directed a play, was blissfully ignorant.

They rehearsed a few times and since there was no script to be "memorized," the students quickly became the characters they were portraying. The result was a forty-minute Thanksgiving celebration and the children spoke in loud, clear, natural voices with no microphones or sound system. The students, speaking the parts they had written, spoke spontaneously onstage about the hardships of their winter, the meeting with Squanto, and the eventual sharing of the feast with the Native Americans.

The bonus came in the classroom after the play was over. The students were in Reading Group Three—the Redbirds. When it came time for Jonah to read in the round-robin circle, he surprised everyone by reading his paragraph with inflection, fluency, and a booming voice. The children who were doing seat-work dropped their pencils. Those Redbirds awaiting their turn to read aloud (a heretofore dreaded experience) sat with their mouths agape and said, "Jonah, when did you learn to read like that?" "Yesterday," he replied. "I figured out some of those words on the flashcards do appear in books and a story is like a play. I just read it like I'm in the play. Being a pilgrim and talking onstage without having to read it made me feel like I was really there and now I know books can make you feel the same way!"

—Gail Brown, teacher, author, and director, Casa Grande, Arizona

✫ What We Learned ✫

By the time Gail moved to Orcas Island in Washington State, the fourth grade play had become a tradition for her. There she met Colleen, who had two daughters. As the daughters moved through elementary school, each participated in the play, and Colleen and Gail always worked together, whether her children were involved or not. That was the beginning of the partnership, and it served us well when we moved on to the adult variety format.

Our first show was done on a tightly stretched shoestring budget. Our understanding of what we were taking on was limited. Honestly, we didn't even have a shoestring. When we needed to purchase items, we charged at the local pharmacy or lumberyard and repaid them after the show was over. We did our shows back in the eighties, so the profits seemed huge at the time. If the show brought in $1,000 to $2,000, that was a success, considering we were previously only bringing in around $50 to $100 or so on car washes, bake sales, and sock hops.

We learned quickly that the challenge was to manage the conflict between control of all the elements behind the curtain and the potential chaos that can strike at any time. That chaos might begin with a performer who doesn't show up or a backdrop that collapses in the middle of the performance. It can happen on Orcas Island, in Phoenix, Arizona, or on Broadway. Be prepared, it will happen to you, and it has happened to all of us. Here's the secret: You have to have faith that your organization and your crew will work it out. As Phillip Henslowe (Geoffrey Rush) says in *Shakespeare in Love*:

> PHILLIP HENSLOWE: Mr. Fennyman, allow me to explain about the theater business. The natural condition is one of insurmountable obstacles on the road to imminent disaster.
> HUGH FENNYMAN: So what do we do?
> PHILIP HENSLOWE: Nothing. Strangely enough, it all turns out well.
> HUGH FENNYMAN: How?
> PHILIP HENSLOWE: I don't know. It's a mystery.

The greatest surprise is that your audience will understand, help pull you through any crisis that may arise, and applaud the success when the show continues to go on. Throughout the book we will share tales of adversity and triumph, experienced by producers in all venues of the theatrical community. These stories are included to help you have understanding, perspective, and a laugh or two at the task we have all chosen. Why? It's a mystery. Have fun!

When you decide to become a co-director for a variety show fundraiser, you will ask yourself, as we asked ourselves, "What am I getting into?" The answer is—a lot! You will spend considerable time and energy to raise funds for a cause you believe in completely. Of course, if we'd had a large amount of disposable income, we could have written a huge check, and gotten on with our lives. We didn't have that option; in fact, most people at the grassroots level involved in a nonprofit organization aren't able to do this. And that's not a bad thing. Simply writing a check means you would miss out on some wonderful, life-changing experiences.

☆ Why a Variety Show? ☆

A variety show is an excellent way to showcase many people. When a group, including people of all ages, comes together to make a one-of-a-kind show, a camaraderie is engendered that is different from using a scripted play. The participants help create the writing, the choreography, the costumes, the sets—every aspect of this unique performance—and they come away with a true sense of ownership.

☆ Why Bother? ☆

Producing a play, a musical, a variety show, or even a simple talent show requires planning, organization, and hard work. The requirements for a fourth-grade school play are nearly the same as a Broadway production. Anyone who has ever been involved in theater at any level knows how much work is involved to produce, promote, and deliver a quality show. As a fourth grade student once said as we were rehearsing a scene for the fifteenth time, "You know what? This isn't a PLAY; it's a WORK!"

However, hard work isn't the whole story. Let's face it, a couple thousand dollars isn't worth the enormous effort, unless the participants are getting something more than money out of it (and of course no individual participant is making a dime, which is true for most participants involved in most levels of theater, even a lot of professional theater). There's got to be a reason why people bust their tails and sacrifice their time to a show, when they could much more easily put a dollar, or a hundred dollars, into an envelope. The reason? People attain personal benefits when they are involved in a special event like a performance, benefits that are often more enriching than cash.

Why do people want to be onstage? They get a sense of fulfillment, and a realization that they have special talents. People often blossom when they are allowed to perform, and find that they have a desire to share their insights and talents with others. Practically every garage band in the world ultimately wants to see its name in lights and become famous. Only a few make it to the top, but many musicians who don't achieve national success, continue expressing themselves in local bistros, at weddings, bar mitzvahs, karaoke clubs, and open mike nights. Most actors who have had a taste of success onstage will continue to perform in high school, college, community theater, and road companies.

Benefits of participation in a local production are not only personal, but extend to others in the theater community. A sense of belonging comes with participation in a troupe or series of shows. Friendships are formed quickly and many romances begin onstage, or backstage. Another great reward is simply to get away from the daily routine. It is fascinating to see the local insurance man, who everyone in town knows works in an office all day wearing a suit and tie, come onstage in a crazy costume and makeup. When he lets go with a right-on rendition of "Hey Jude," he loves it, the crowd loves it and maybe he sells a policy to a new customer on Monday morning.

Financial success rewards those who make it to the next level, but the satisfaction of seeing your work as a volunteer contribute to a worthy cause is priceless. Nowadays, nonprofits have come on tough times and raising money is difficult with the cutbacks in government program grants. Economic conditions and competition have made fundraising more important than ever. The bonding experience of creating a show together will also create a loyal group of volunteers. Consistent loyalty and support is the lifeblood of nonprofit and community-based organizations.

☆ The People Out There Who Can Help ☆

When you take on a job like directing, you are creating and managing a mini-universe where every detail is your responsibility. It may seem overwhelming, but don't be discouraged, there are people out there who can help you. Every community has theater people who want to perform and promote a production. They will work onstage, backstage, and out front. Seek them out. Most are easy to find. They have experience and know what they are doing. Call your local college or community theater and let them know what you are planning to do. Ask if they have people who would like to join in or offer advice. Most teachers are interested in performing or have ideas that can lead to others who are excited about being onstage or working behind the scenes.

Citizens with a special talent or connection may be thrilled to help out. We knew a local hairdresser who had been involved in theater during high school. She was delighted to teach novice actors to apply makeup and recreate hairstyles from past eras.

Remember the "six degrees of separation" theory that says anyone on earth can be connected to any other person on earth through a chain of acquaintances? Almost everyone knows someone who knows someone and that can lead to a celebrity. If you include a celebrity in your show, his or her status could mean an increase in ticket sales and often leads to some hefty donations to your cause.

Jim Youngren was a close friend of Emmy Lou Harris and brought her to the island to record an album. She agreed to put on an impromptu concert at the local Grange Hall one night. It was supposed to be hush-hush, but by 8:00 that evening, the word had gotten out, the parking lot was overflowing, and a line of people extended from the front door down the road a mile and a half to the recycling center. The performance did not need flyers, radio spots, or commercials. Once the word got out, almost everyone on the island knew about it in a couple of hours.

Since Orcas, though small, was an attractive boating and tourist destination for the whole of the West Coast, and many "celebrities" had summer homes there, we did consider seeking them out to perform in our shows, but decided to use only local talent. At that time, we did not want to direct the focus to the celebrities, but if available, they would certainly add spice to your show. Either choice is good, depending on your philosophy and overall goal.

While we stayed away from celebrities, we certainly didn't hesitate to seek out people who had extensive experience in the theater. Thelma Swan McTavish was a theater person and her rendition of Charlie Chaplin in June Schulberg's "Bicentennial Extravaganza" was spot-on. With her bowler hat, cane, and tiny moustache, she brought Charlie to life before our very eyes. Once everyone knew she was a Chaplin fan, gift giving became easy. When someone found a poster, figurine, or decorated box they were quickly added to her extensive memorabilia collection. A full size poster hangs inside the door of her guest bathroom and it is often disconcerting to step out of the shower and see the Little Tramp staring at you (before realizing its just an artist's rendering, not a real human being!) Thelma worked with us on several of our shows, always adding something unique and exciting.

Another important group, however, is people who have never participated but discover the fun of the stage when they are invited to join. They are able, hardworking "helpers" and business people who will donate to funding, organizing, advertising, construction, and just plain schlepping. They will drive a pickup truck to move a 200-pound desk at 8:00 at night, or hem a costume five minutes before show time. Many of these people have undiscovered talents that will be exposed when brought to the theater. Wes Pomeroy, a local teacher, was able to construct anything from doorways to puppet theaters. A request would be made and within two days, his creations would appear ready to be used. When we first approached him, we had no idea that his talent in this area was so extensive. Wes was deliberate and methodical. Rehearsals would be over, we would be ready to leave after teaching all day followed by a two-hour rehearsal, and he would still be working on a support for a wobbly flat. The next day we would return and find the support in place and a flat you couldn't move with a bulldozer. If we were expecting a "regular" doorframe, he constructed the perfect door. He taught math the same way and we all loved him.

If you are fortunate enough to have a group of experienced actors, artists, and musicians, of course it will be easier to produce a show because they have done it all before. But even if all you have to start with is a group with absolutely no theater background, as you work on your first show together, you will begin to build your pool of experienced and dedicated theater artists!

☆ Co-directors ☆

In real-life terms, the "head" jobs usually fall into two nominal areas: the director and the producer. The director generally manages artistic content, artists, music, and the overall look and feel of the show. In commercial theater, the producer is usually the person responsible for overseeing the practical details of a show: getting the financing, making sure staff positions are filled, making sure that all aspects of the necessary stagecraft and offstage business are carried out according to a production calendar. The producer at the level we're talking about here is responsible for many of the same areas, but instead of delegating all the jobs to staff, she may well find herself overseeing the sound, backdrops, props, etc., as well as writing the schedule, and corralling a volunteer staff and putting it through its paces.

We suggest two directors, one supervising the onstage activities and one the offstage business, as it is too much work for one person. It is more enjoyable and productive when you have two people who are equally dedicated to the production of the show, and, of course, many responsibilities will overlap. Choose a partner you can work with. One who has enthusiasm, energy, complementary talents, a positive connection to the community, a "can-do" attitude, and a good sense of humor.

When we worked together, we knew we got along well and would be productive. We also knew that Colleen was good at organizing and getting people excited about the program, whereas Gail had more experience in casting and directing. That meant Colleen took care of keeping everyone on track and assuring all bases were covered while Gail was more interested in finding someone who looked like John Travolta. Colleen had a notebook with colored tabs and kept all pertinent information in alphabetical order. Gail was more likely to stuff phone numbers in her huge carryall and wasted a considerable amount of time retrieving information. It was obvious early on that Colleen would be the one to keep track of meetings and rehearsals as she had access to everyone's home number at her fingertips. Gail spent more time working with the staging and direction.

We chose to call ourselves co-directors rather than director and producer because we shared so many responsibilities and we both wanted to be available to respond to all crises—artistic and otherwise—as they came up. This probably wasn't the best division of labor, but most of our enjoyment came from critiquing acts, choosing people to play certain parts, and co-solving the many problems as they arose. We both knew we were equally responsible for the final production and preferred to stick together throughout the process. After one show, we had T-shirts made saying, "We'll take the flak."

Above all, the co-directors must know the purpose for working long hours and be willing to do it for little or no financial reward. (The less you spend, the more you make.) Both will know the joy that comes from uniting a diverse group of people in a common goal and producing a quality product.

Good directors for this kind of project are people who are inclusive rather than exclusive. They are able to see the talents in each volunteer and give all of them jobs at which they can be successful. Your enthusiasm will generate energy and cooperation from the volunteers.

One of the most difficult issues you will face is the need to be sensitive to community and group standards. The "community" may be a church congregation, a mobile home park, or a small town. The directors are responsible for knowing what is appropriate and inappropriate for the audience. Above all, they must be insightful enough to recognize the boundaries and strong enough to insist that the boundaries be adhered to.

Sometimes, things happen before the co-directors know they are going to be problematic. We had one musician arrive late after a trip to the local tavern and we didn't notice he had taken on a few more than he should have. As he was onstage, it became clearly apparent he was not in top form, so we actually used a theater "hook" to remove him. The audience thought it was all part of the act, so we used it again the following night when he arrived early, sober, and prepared. The "hook" added an old-time vaudeville tone and no one in the audience knew what had transpired.

Directors want everything to go just right. That is their job: take a chaotic universe and make it function perfectly. However, grown-up people have minds of their own, and the variety show format encourages creativity and individual talent. Sometimes, they will cross the line of propriety and once the act is onstage, there is no way the directors can control the performers except use the hook.

Know your audience. Be sensitive to situations and humor that might offend or hurt. Remember that you cannot please everyone. Some of your performers may have a different sense of what is acceptable and what is not acceptable than you do. As directors, you will have to be tactful, but certain in your decisions. Co-directors have the "final say" in what is presented to the audience. Freedom of speech stops where the audience begins. You are not onstage to send a message, but to gather support and raise funds for a cause everyone agrees on. Hurting or offending someone is not only unnecessary, it is unacceptable.

One prospective performer wanted to play his guitar and sing a popular song that included two words that the directors deemed inappropriate. After much discussion, the singer reluctantly agreed to change the words so it wouldn't be offensive to the audience. He promised to do that and thankfully, he kept his word.

Patience, humor, enthusiasm, understanding of the goal, clear communication, knowing how much money is needed to complete the project, and how much profit is needed to make the time and effort spent worthwhile, are all important.

Characteristics of Co-directors

- Dedicated to the goals
- Enthusiastic
- Well known (and respected) in the community or organization
- Willing to work for the joy of the experience
- Organized
- Sensitive, yet able to make tough decisions
- Able to interact with people from all walks of life
- Inclusive rather than exclusive
- Enjoys meeting new people and doing something different
- Willing to see problems as challenges instead of roadblocks
- Able to delegate responsibilities

☆ Under Whose Auspices? ☆

When we got the brilliant idea to put on a show, we weren't working under the auspices of a specific organization. We just did it. Since the Orcas Center was just starting up, we worked on our own and donated the proceeds to the local Booster Club, a school support group for athletics and activities. Velma Doty, president, collected the money, designated it for the building and kept it in a separate account. This account provided us with seed money for the following year, but we never used much for production costs. The community donated time and materials as needed. As years passed, it became necessary to pay for some costumes, sound equipment, and props, but by that time, we had enough funds to get what we needed. Even then, the cash demands were low due to the generosity of the community.

As times have changed, the Center has become a real business. Today all transactions, including the budget, would have to adhere to written guidelines. It is highly improbable that any group today would be able to "just do it." Keep this in mind and get approval from sponsoring organization before starting on your volunteer venture.

The Orcas Center for the Arts is now a nonprofit corporation and any fundraiser has to be presented to the board of directors for approval. Today, there are so many shows and events, the board has to be selective about what can or cannot be presented under its auspices. The calendar fills up quickly and some tough decisions have to be made about what to include or exclude.

When the Lions Club or the Medical Center produces a show, a proposal must be presented in writing for the board's consideration. It is no longer an option to just fly by the seat of your pants with no group or organization to support your venture.

Although it may be disappointing that you can't just go out and re-invent the wheel, there are many advantages to working under the auspices of a sponsoring organization. If your community trusts the sponsoring group, the association could help you build an audience. The audience benefits if you do your fundraising through a nonprofit organization, because that makes their donations tax deductible. In addition, working under the umbrella of a nonprofit organization could mean that you don't have to pay sales tax on anything you need to buy for your show.

Some groups, such as sororities or fraternities, have an annual tradition of presenting a talent show, in which case it might be easier to produce the show. Most churches, schools, or service organizations get their volunteers and talent from their own group. This makes the process easier than drawing from a whole community or a large city. If you don't have a set group, much more time and effort will be spent recruiting talent.

☆ Getting Organized: Who You Need and What You Need ☆

Once you have decided you are going to work together, what do you do? In addition to acts and performers onstage, you will need many volunteers for preproduction jobs and behind-the-scenes positions. It is important to realize that theater is not only the group of grown-up people in makeup and costumes playing make-believe. The crew that supports them must be practical, technically skilled, flexible, and able to produce real-life solutions at a moment's notice. Your job is to find these people.

Committed volunteers are critical in making the show a success, but not everyone has to donate the same amount of time. Many will be required to spend a great deal of time and others may only need to show up for dress rehearsal and performance nights. The following is a list of general areas for which you need to find leaders. Each is discussed in detail in the relevant chapters.

Areas of Responsibility

* **Cast**
* **Backstage Crew**
* **Stage Manager:** Someone who can do everything
* **Scriptwriters:** Good writers who can write comedy
* **Financial and Legal Issues:** Do not overlook these areas
* **Database and History:** You'll need someone not only dedicated, but also detail-oriented
* **Publicity/Design/Tickets:** A smart designer is necessary
* **Musicians:** May be difficult to round up, but invaluable if you get the right ones
* **Construction/Lighting/Sound:** People to do any design, building, light hanging, and other pre-show tech work, plus work with stage crew to make it work
* **Front End:** Ushers, ticket takers, cashiers, concessions
* **Miscellaneous:** Cleanup, gofers, and other details

After agreeing to be co-directors, we immediately began to identify and solicit a small group of writers to develop the script. We decided on the variety show format, knew we wanted to localize the content, and began looking for bright, witty people who were either new and had a fresh perspective on island living, or island natives who knew the crazy stories of times gone by; skeletons could be pulled out of the closet and safely subjected to a little humor. Since the creative process was more organic than directed, we had to rely on the people we selected and the material that came out of living on a resort island in the middle of a tremendous growth spurt, with lots of history and personalities. We will deal more with the specifics of the process in chapter 10, "Writing Your Script."

When we did our first show, we got our idea, found our volunteers, and then we decided upon dates and venue. Depending upon the size of the show you are planning, and the organization you are planning it for, you may not approach your "to do" list in that order. You may have to choose your dates before you put your team together, because of your organization's schedule, or the availability of an attractive venue, or because of a community concern. As you'll hear later, our community's calendar ultimately dictated when it was best for us to produce our show.

Select a venue, choose a date, make a time line, and tend to all other physical and mechanical aspects that support onstage success. ALLOW PLENTY OF LEAD TIME! This is an important consideration and one that people—experienced or inexperienced—tend to overlook. In theater, of course, there is never enough time, and yet, strangely, the show always goes on. When we first started, we allowed ourselves four months to get the show together. That schedule worked for the second and third shows as well.

☆ The Right Tool for the Job ☆

You, as the co-directors, will be responsible for finding the right people for each job. Perhaps people have told you they want to be involved in some way, or they have an act that is already being done or is inappropriate, but still want to help. Draw from this pool first. Good co-directors listen to all suggestions, as it is important to be open to new ideas. Listening generates creativity and a commitment to the project. Suggestions that enrich a show can come from many different quarters. One of the women working on costumes came up with an idea to have someone dressed in period costume to hold signs saying Act One, Intermission, Act Two, and The End. The next year one of the construction crew suggested having a couple on roller skaters hold the signs (also a good little tip to get young, hesitant students onstage).

The co-directors are the captains of the ship and have the final word. They have the combined experience to decide what will and will not work (or, maybe, the first time you do this you don't have the experience, but let's hope you have the combined intuition and confidence). The show *American Idol* provides us with many horrendous examples of people who believe they have talent in a certain area, but who clearly should find another way to direct their energy. If such misguided individuals offer their talents, rather than reject them, diplomatically steer them toward a different task. Volunteers are the backbone of this event, the team that makes it happen.

☆ Vision Statement ☆

A vision statement will help you clarify what your group wants to accomplish for the long run. In addition, it will help guide you and keep you on track to achieving the goal. The vision statement is a statement of your "vision" for the future–where would you like to be in five years? What would be the ideal fulfillment of goals for the organization? Draw from the goals and values of your organization and its surrounding community. The vision statement will help guide you to the projects that correspond to, support, and achieve that long-term vision. For example, if you want to build a new performing arts center, a variety show is a specific project that will help you raise money to reach that goal. Clarity is the key.

☆ Mission Statement ☆

When you know where you are going and can state it explicitly, people will be drawn to your project. That is why it is important to write a mission statement for your group that focuses on your immediate goal. Make it short and direct. You want your crew and community to know where their hard work and money are going and why. The statement will focus your artistic ideas, help recruit volunteers, direct the writing, and shape promotional activities. Explain why you need to raise money and collect in-kind donations in twenty words or less and use that idea when asking for project contributions. You can create a short simple mission statement by giving specific answers to three basic questions:

* *Who are we*? Clearly identify your organization.
* *What are we doing*? Clearly identify the project.
* *What is the purpose*? Explain why you are raising money.

For example: "The Orcas Education Foundation is putting on a variety show at Rosario Resort to raise money to start a fund for a community theater."

Once you have a clear statement, much of the publicity language will be clarified. This will help your designer work your message into the design and image package. Whether you are doing a flyer, poster, or TV ad, you can fall back on this language to guide you. For example, an elementary school that has "Success for All" as its primary focus would reflect this as the overall theme of their show.

☆ A Word of Caution: Starting "Everything" at Once ☆

When you start, a number of things must be done simultaneously. We have to deal with them sequentially in the context of a book. Searching for a venue, writing, finding acts, initiating design and publicity, all need to begin around the same time. You will have to organize these jobs in accordance with your situation and who is available. If you have an auditorium with a stage, kitchen, and foyer, you simply need to reserve it for rehearsals and performances. If you are a member of an organization with an image package and a logo, you can get going on publicity posters, flyers, and preliminary work on a program. Just allow as much lead time as possible for every job, particularly publicity and printing.

CHAPTER 2

Volunteers

Volunteers make it possible for community theater projects and fundraising to work. They give their time to attain a goal with the least possible financial outlay. People love to be asked and they want to display their talents.

☆ Stories from the Stage ☆

At one time, I was in dire need of new and exciting ideas for raising a lot of money to support the theater. The volunteers kept promising to come up with something and time was growing short. I called an emergency meeting of all volunteers. After the sandwiches and coffee were delivered, I calmly walked over to the door, locked it tight, turned around with my back up against the door and said, "No one is leaving this room until we come up with twenty-five new ideas!" It worked!

—*Thelma McTavish, a pint-sized person with a gigantic personality,*
is the fundraiser extraordinaire for The Village Theatre
in Issaquah, Washington

☆ Another Story from the Stage ☆

Cornerstone Theater was touring the country with a contemporary adaptation of a Shakespeare play we called The Winter's Tale: An Interstate Adventure. *We always found a clunker car in every town in which we were performing. I would make my entrance in the clunker, do the scene, and then drive offstage. However, in one particular performance, the car would not start. Before the stage-crew members could respond, three guys from the audience jumped onstage, got behind the car and pushed it offstage. They turned, ran back to their seats, and sat down. The audience gave them a big hand and the show continued. You never know where the next volunteer is going to show up.*

—*Christopher Liam Moore, actor, director, and founding member, Cornerstone Theater Company, Los Angeles*

✯ What We Did ✯

The population of our island was around two thousand in the early days of the show. Every event from the Library Fair to Casino Night at the "Legion" to the Christmas Bazaar in the school gym had a great group of volunteers. Their bona fides were established and you knew whom you could count on. The population was so small on the island that everyone knew the hard workers and the poor souls who couldn't say no. We think it's fair to assume that all communities, large and small, come with a similar talent pool. You just have to find the right people. Volunteers are willing and eager to devote time and labor to a cause they believe in. On Orcas, many stepped forward as soon as they heard what we were doing. Others we contacted and some, like the Sha Na Na group, were simply corralled.

Here are some of things we did, and some of the people we approached, in order to round up our volunteers the first year we did the variety show. We knew a hairdresser who had been involved in theater and she volunteered to lead the hair and makeup crew, two local construction workers were asked to build the stage and sets, and some high school students we had worked with volunteered to do the lighting. Since many shows had been staged on Orcas over the years, the actors were asked to reprise some of their favorite acts from the old days or come up with new ideas. It was a treat for the older members to see Cherie Lindholm Carlson and her partner reprise their dancing horse routine from twenty years earlier!

We had a team of thirty core people working to put the show up with team leaders, backstage crew, and lighting and sound technicians. Our final count totaled ninety-two people involved onstage, behind the scenes, and general support. Although many of these people made only small contributions and watched the show as part of the audience, they were included in the program "Thank You" list.

A friend who lived in Seattle wanted to do a show and was afraid it would be too difficult to find people in such a large city who would want to be involved. Her goal was to raise money for an animal shelter. When she began talking to the people in her neighborhood, she found that even though Seattle is large, there are small communities within the city. She went to pet shops, veterinarians, pet groomers, and dog show enthusiasts to find those who shared her love of animals. Before she knew it, she had fifty volunteers.

Her theme was "Shelter from the Storm" and included renditions of "Stormy Weather," "Don't Rain on my Parade," and "Singin' in the Rain" (Remember she was in Seattle!) and a variety of acts that had nothing to do with rain or shelters but raised lots of money for the cause.

☆ What We Learned ☆

In all organizations—churches, schools, charities—many are already contributing and others are eager to help. Certain people who are experts in specific areas will come to mind. Contact these people for specific jobs. Give them clear details about what the project will entail, including your goals and the amount of time they will have to spend. They will enlist. Many of these people will be right for leadership positions. Most will have a group of people they can call on to network with, including friends and associates, to expand the volunteer pool. The fact is, even in large cities, specialized communities exist such as school groups and service clubs. Think of Seattle's dog-loving population discussed above. You will simply need to reach out, explain your project, and people will respond. Visit local Parent-Teacher Organizations, put out flyers, or go to the organization in the local retirement, or "fifty-five-plus," community.

One community theater group, Cornerstone Theater Company, has been extremely successful in identifying and seeking-out unique "communities." For example, they are working with Native American tribes on reservations, finding people interested in theater in inner cities, and currently creating a group in the local legal community from judges to police to inmates.

If certain jobs seem too overwhelming and don't work into people's schedules, in most cases they will probably ask if there is another job they can do. Don't be shy. If they don't ask, you ask them. The initial phone calls are important as the volunteers will pick up on your passion; enthusiasm is contagious.

☆ Volunteers' First Meeting ☆

You or your co-director should keep track of what jobs you need filled, and what volunteers you have solicited. Because of our inclusive approach, we solicited a lot of volunteers. We had a good idea how we were going to use some of them; others we figured we'd find a place as the project rolled along. Once we'd done this for a while, we had a clearer sense of what jobs were going to crop up, and we became better at assigning people tasks right from the get-go. Look at the jobs in the list on the following pages and modify the list to suit your situation.

First Meeting

Set up a meeting for the co-directors and team leaders. Once you set the date, don't change it. There will always be someone who would like to switch it from Tuesday to Saturday. Pick a date that suits the most people and stick with it. You need to remain firm about schedules for a couple of reasons. Number one, you will never be able to get every-thing done if you waffle a lot. Two, volunteers all have lives of their own, but they must understand that this show is a commitment, too, and they need to try to be available when the show requires their par-ticipation. Ask every team leader to attend the meeting, as it will be the first, and perhaps, the only, one of its kind. Other meetings will take place with smaller groups, but this first meeting brings all team leaders together so they can receive the pertinent information at one time and questions can be answered. (Refer to the sample outline for the first meeting in appendix B.)

Have notebooks prepared for every team leader. Each team leader is put in charge of a specific task, or set of tasks, that he or she is particularly suited for, and is responsible for finding people to work on the team. Many associated responsibilities could be delegated to one group and managed by one team leader. For example, in our group, the mechanical jobs usually became the responsibility of one of the carpenters or electricians. Often the lead hairdresser managed makeup and costume.

The notebooks (one-and-one-half inch binders with tabbed sec-tions) should include:

- **First page:** Vision statement, mission statement, sponsoring organ-ization, and gratitude note from the co-directors
- **Tab One:** Contact sheet with team leaders and directors' names, phone numbers, and e-mail addresses
- **Tab Two:** Contact sheet with team members' names, phone num-bers, and e-mail addresses
- **Tab Three:** Meeting and rehearsal schedules
- **Tab Four:** Expense sheets with pockets for receipts
- **Tab Five:** Team checklist
- **Remaining Tabs:** Leave blank to be used at leader's discretion

The co-directors ask each team leader to pass on to their volunteers exactly what is expected, how much time they are being asked to donate, and the personal benefits they will gain. The team leaders are responsible for having an initial meeting and subsequent meetings with their team. Team leaders should send regular e-mail updates on the progress of the group. When we did our shows, there was no e-mail, so we kept in touch by telephone and impromptu meetings when we bumped into one another at the store or around the village. Today, e-mail certainly makes it easier to stay on top of what is getting done and who is doing it.

☆ Taking Care of Business ☆

The following is a list of "jobs to be done" more than "positions to be filled." Often, one or two people will assume a number of responsibilities. You will not need to fill all these positions. Modify the descriptions to suit your show's needs and the talents of your volunteers. Encourage your team leader to decide how many people are needed to complete these tasks. Many operating groups may have some positions already filled by staff members.

Some of these jobs may not seem that critical. Having people to build the stage and perform acts upon it may at first seem far, far more important than finding someone to provide child care. Certainly building a stage is going to require more volunteer time than will babysitting for two hours. However, at the critical moment, when the curtain's about to go up, and you've got a bunch of over-excited kids backstage, you will be thankful that you found someone willing to "wrangle" the kids.

Carpenters

The **carpenter team leader** is responsible for the construction of the necessary sets for the overall theme, and individual acts if necessary. This job may require stage modification or erecting a full stage depending on the venue chosen. This team is a group of carpenters or handymen with experience. For any job from the main stage sets to acts that needs something constructed, these people will get it done.

Cast

The gathering and rehearsing of the cast is the responsibility of the co-directors. The cast itself, of course, is responsible for providing the entertainment.

Cast Party

The **cast party team leader** locates the site for the party, plans food and beverages (generally a potluck), sets up, cleans up, and helps celebrate this happy occasion. This may not seem like a really important event, but it's a nice "thank you" to your cast. Also, without it, the cast often feels that the experience is incomplete. A party kind of puts a button on it.

Child Sitters

The **child sitter team leader** is responsible for finding three or four people (preferably school teacher types) who can provide entertainment for the children backstage and help with children in the audience.

Cleanup

The **cleanup team leader** makes certain your venue is left in the same condition in which it was received after each show, and especially after the final show. The team leader is probably going to have to ask volunteers to wear two hats (that is, even though the grunge band performed onstage, you might need to ask the future alternative music stars to help you take out the trash). Of course there is always the old-school teacher maxim: "I don't care who dropped it. If it is on the floor, pick it up. We all live here." We always found that everyone just pitched in, and before we knew it, everything was spick and span. A crew with a pickup or van may need to return the next morning to remove the larger items.

Concessions

A **concessions team leader** is needed if you plan to serve or sell refreshments during intermission.

Database

The **database team leader** sets up a mass-mailing e-mail list and keeps a record of all individuals, suppliers, and contacts involved in the show. The mass-mailing database list is used for communication to the entire cast and crew, and is a direct contact to next year's audience, suppliers, and volunteers.

Finances

The **financial director** assists the co-directors in preparing a financial pro forma. He or she works directly with anyone spending or receiving funds. The financial director prepares a finished report after all income and expenses are accounted for. This report is available to the public. Share your success! Most clubs, organizations, theater groups, or churches will have a person who is already part of the staff. If, for some reason, you do not have a built-in financial advisor, look for someone in the community who is experienced in this area. The financial director asks each of the team leaders what costs may be incurred to complete their tasks. *Everything you find, borrow, create, or is donated builds your bottom line*. Financial accountings of the ticket sales are sent to the financial director on an ongoing basis. This person prepares a financial accounting the week following the show to be distributed to the board of your organization and other appropriate parties. Most people simply ask, "How much money did we make?" There are others who will want to see the show's financial report.

Graphic Design

Someone with design and printing experience should head graphic design, if possible. Involve him or her from the beginning. The **graphic design team leader** is responsible for designing all marketing material, including flyers, posters, tickets, newspaper ads, and the program, and for working with printers. If your program is under the auspices of an existing nonprofit organization, you may want or need to integrate existing company logo and graphics with your promotional materials. This is a specialized area and it is up to the team leader to decide how many people he or she would like to include. Printing savvy can save you much money. For example, one- or two-color printing on a muted tone stock can yield a classy program without the expense of full color and glossy paper. The directors must approve all material. Take your time on the final press proof.

House Manager and Ushers

The **house manager** organizes the **ushers**, who welcome guests, pass out programs, show people to their seats, coordinate the opening of the theater doors at the appropriate times and are generally available to fill in when the need arises.

Hairdressers

The **hairdresser team leader** can be a local hairdresser. He or she is responsible for procuring wigs, hairpieces, mustaches, beards, combs, brushes, and is available for consultation with different acts. A team of three or four hairdressers is sufficient.

Historian

The **historian** keeps a running scrapbook of all marketing materials, photos, and any other pertinent items. These will be useful when you plan next year's show.

Legal

For all legal issues, use a lawyer. The best choice to help with your financial questions and budget is a CPA because he or she will be able to point out important tax situations, insurance risks, and direct you to get legal advice when appropriate.

Lighting

Experience is extremely valuable in this area. The **lighting team leader** will need to create a lighting plan that will provide overall illumination for all the acts that will occur and will also have to deal with any "specials" such as follow spots, different colored lights, screen projections, etc. He or she will have to plan where the lights need to go in order to get maximum value out of the "instruments." (That's what the lights are called. The plan is called a "plot.") He or she will also need to pull a crew together to hang and focus any rented or borrowed instruments—and take them down again when the show is over. If the venue has a computer lighting board, he or she will need to know how to program it, and how to train someone to run it. If the lighting is of a less sophisticated type, he or she will have to know how to get maximum benefit out of it. This person solves all lighting challenges—and there will be many!

You need good lighting people because each site has its own set of challenges. A professional lighting person will be able to assess the venue, make a list of things needed, and will know where to find equipment. In order to plan the lighting, the lighting team leader will need a specific sheet from the co-directors that lists each act's individual lighting requirements. Obviously, the co-directors will need to know exactly what each act has planned in order to provide that information, which is one of the reasons why watching rehearsals and talking to your performers is so important. However, if the co-directors do not feel comfortable coming up with this list, try to get your lighting expert to watch rehearsals, or at least give him or her a very good idea of what is going to be happening on the stage. Think about a lighting board, spotlights, footlights, black lights, floodlights, robo-lights, reflective lights, spinning balls, and perhaps most importantly, ample electrical outlets. You may need to borrow some of the items from the local theater, high school, or college drama department. You may find that local venues do not own the lights you need, and you will have to rent them from a lighting rental house. You will need to look through local listings for suppliers, or else ask your community theater or other entertainment venue from whom they rent.

Makeup

The **makeup artist team leader** should have experience and/or definite artistic talent. This person must secure all makeup, brushes, mirrors, and the like to be used when performing this job. Makeup stations have to be available so several people can be made up simultaneously. In a variety show, some people choose to do their own makeup, while others require full makeup from a professional. After you have received cast requirements for makeup you can determine the number of makeup artists needed.

Moving Crew

The **moving crew team leader** oversees the pickup and delivery to the site of all large items that are needed for the show. They also return these to the appropriate owner after the show.

Music

The **music team leader** (often referred to as the music director) will help ensure overall music quality. This person works closely with the co-directors. He or she may select band members, assist acts as needed, schedule band rehearsals, and direct music at dress rehearsals and show nights. This person assists in musical selections, researches royalties, and works closely with the sound team leader. These positions go hand in hand to produce a high-quality show.

Photographer

The **photography team leader** can be a professional or novice who is interested in chronicling the show's journey from beginning to end with color and black-and-white images. Decide who is going to pay for film and developing photos and who owns the negatives after the show is over. If photos are digital, arrange for photo paper, printing, and perhaps, creating CDs to sell.

Props

The **prop team leader**, is responsible for securing and managing all props. During the show the leader or a member of props team will act as prop manager, making sure that there is a well-managed prop table backstage—where performers can pick up or put down props as they go on- and offstage—and a place where props can be stored. Many acts will provide their own props. The prop team leader makes certain all props are gathered and returned to the rightful owners.

Publicity

The **publicity team leader** promotes the show. Experience in the area of publicity is necessary. He works closely with the graphic designer. He will write press releases (or see to it that someone does). He will have or locate the contact information needed to ensure that publicity materials end up in the hands of people who can push the show. This is an area where a staff member who is a public relations or human resources person can help.

Scriptwriters

The co-directors should select all members of the writing team. The writers are responsible for writing a tight script based on the theme chosen by the organization, with jokes and references tailored to your particular community.

Sound

The **sound team leader** is responsible for the sound equipment and setup. He or she assists in determining the sound needs of the room such as microphones, headsets, piano mikes, cables, speakers, and soundboards. This person will make sure that this equipment is procured, properly installed, and disassembled and returned to whence it came after the show is over. The leader, or a member of the crew, in tandem with the stage manager, will make sure that equipment is in working order before the top of the show.

Stage Crew

The **stage crew team leader** must find people to move scenery, provide special effects, and do pre-show prep such as sweeping, mopping, and generally getting the venue ready for the performance. On the days of the performance, the leader and the crew, just like the sound crew, lighting crew, performers, makeup people, ushers, etc., will work under the direction of the stage manager.

Stage Manager

The **stage manager (SM)** needs to be a strong leader, a good communicator, and very detail-oriented. This job can be very involved and time-consuming, and you will need someone dedicated.

The SM serves as an assistant to the director, and attends all rehearsals. He or she will probably even attend rehearsals of the individual acts (along with the director), and will definitely be in communication with the performers of those acts, because the SM must keep a list of all of the items that each act requires—and will also be responsible for keeping track of how long the show is running. The SM, under the supervision of the director, usually creates a special script that lists the acts with all technical and performer cues clearly marked. During the big rehearsals—such as the technical rehearsal and the dress rehearsals—and the actual performances, the SM "calls" the show; that is, he or she lets all performers know when they are supposed to be ready to go onstage, and also alerts crew people as to when they have to bring up the lights, or change the furniture, etc. In many theaters, the SM and the other backstage team leaders will wear headsets so they can talk to each other without having to run around backstage and without the audience hearing. But a lot of shoestring shows have gotten by without that technology. See appendix D for helpful texts about stage management.

Ticket Sales

The **ticket sales team leader** is responsible for a financial accounting of all tickets sold. This person oversees and keeps an accounting of every ticket available for sale. He or she distributes tickets to appropriate sales locations and manages the ticket sales team, including business owners and people at various locations designated as ticket outlets. These days there are many different ways for selling, distributing, and even for printing and keeping track of ticket sales. The size and the backing of your organization (are you working under the auspices of a nonprofit? A school? Or are you going it alone?) and the venue where you are presenting (a four-hundred seat theater with a designated box office, or a sixty-seat, "black box" cabaret in a basement) may alter the tools you have available to you (ticketing software? Credit card machine?) and the way in which you run things.

Video Crew

An experienced **video crew team leader** records some rehearsals, dress rehearsal, and one or two performances. She shoots testimonials from cast and crew throughout production and audience comments after the show that can be used in a marketing campaign or on your Web site.

Wardrobe

The **wardrobe team leader** is full of artistic talent and is able to come up with costume ideas that enhance the performance. This team leader is available for consultations with performers and will coordinate seamstresses and craftspeople if your show is very ambitious and you want to create costumes from scratch (or even dress up "found" costumes, using a glue gun and some sequins). He or she will definitely make sure there is someone or several someones backstage during the performance who can take responsibility for costumes, dressing actors during quick changes, and repairing costumes damaged during the performance. On this team, the following skilled persons are needed: seamstresses, alterations people, costume designers, and a great scrounger for searching out fabric, fur, hats, boas, wigs, canes, or any specialty items needed by the cast. Depending upon how many times you present the show, and over how long a period of time, the wardrobe people might also take responsibility for laundering or dry cleaning costumes.

Webmaster

The **Webmaster** can work with your graphic designer to create a Web page to implement online ticket sales. This would probably not be feasible if you are operating on a small budget. However, if your organization already has a Web presence, you may want the Webmaster to add a special page or link on the events calendar.

☆ **Plan and Organize** ☆

This list may look like too much to handle before you even start. However, every group gets most of these jobs done in every project they take on without even knowing they are doing so. When we started we didn't know what we were getting ourselves into, but we somehow got through the list. In fact, we only learned that there was a definable list of jobs by going through it, and we hope you can benefit from our experience. This list is designed to help you organize and plan before you get involved. (There will still be surprises.) Large organizations with massive productions break down tasks to this level. If your production requires it, and you have the manpower, go for it. Smaller groups don't, and they get it done anyway. The secret: one person does many jobs. Collect similar jobs together and one person will take responsibility. Dickey Badgley always managed our stage and she also worked with costumes, hair, and props. Norris Wood usually ran the mechanical crew and he understood the whole system so he could advise the lighting and sound guys. In addition, if you needed him for hauling, toting, or fixing, he was there. As we said earlier, this is a list of jobs to do, not required positions to be filled.

CHAPTER 3

Choosing a Date and Venue

Finding a room with a stage and adequate seating and equipment can be a challenge. Often you have to take whatever is available and improvise. One important thing over which you have more control is your schedule. Be sure you allow plenty of time to organize and do a great job.

☆ Stories from the Stage ☆

I remember having to switch venues after all the tickets were printed. I considered re-printing the tickets, which would have been quite expensive, but came up with a better idea. My group and I contacted all the people who had received tickets to sell and told them of the change. They marked out the old venue address and printed labels that were put on the back of each ticket telling the location of the new venue. A creative spin was put on the whole thing by explaining how excited they were to get this less costly and more intimate venue—the one they had wanted in the first place!

—Heidi Simon, events planner, Wilsonville, Oregon

☆ What We Did ☆

When we started in the early seventies producing plays with elementary and high school students, we had few, if any, places to do a show. The local theater group used the old Grange Hall, and sometimes the Seaview Theatre, the local movie theater. The Grange was eighty years old, seated about a hundred people and had a great kitchen, which held more people than the auditorium. Since there were no dressing rooms, costume changes were made in the kitchen. The hall did have a stage with old velvet curtains, but no sound or lighting to speak of, although the acoustics were great. When we used the Grange Hall for high school plays, the audience sat in folding chairs, usually set up two hours before curtain time. Because the building was so old, the wiring was not adequate, the lighting board was faulty, and the lights were old and failing. We used the available equipment up to its capabilities, then borrowed professional equipment and improvised where necessary. We used the Grange over the school gym for a number of reasons. The auditorium was small and intimate and it had great acoustics, which made for great interaction.

The local movie theater, on the other hand, was fifties "modern" and had a large stage, seated 200 people, but was not outfitted for live performances. Again, the wings were small, lighting and sound facilities limited, and it had no real dressing rooms. We used them both and were grateful to have them. The difference was that the Grange was virtually free and the theater had to be reimbursed for lost revenues on all weekend nights. Of course, the school gym had a stage with dressing rooms and ample wings, but lighting was limited. In addition, the gym was often scheduled for athletic practices until eight or nine o'clock at night. The stage acted as the storage area for weight-lifting equipment throughout the year, and since it was built like a barn with extremely high ceilings, acoustics were lousy and a big audience filled only half the building.

☆ What We Learned ☆

The three key things in choosing a location are availability, seating, and cost. You must account for lead time, since, no matter how well you plan, you will always have too much to do and not enough time. You need to locate a venue as soon as possible, since the restrictions of the location will dictate many of your operational decisions.

☆ Location ☆

First, locate places that can accommodate your show. A good, capable crew will help you do this no matter what the problem. The primary challenges, as indicated above, will fall into lighting, sound, stage setup, and dressing. Whatever shortcomings you find will be overcome or worked around. Try to decide which venues offer the most benefits with the least liabilities. For example, we were always most worried about sound and microphones, so we would sacrifice dressing rooms for acoustics every time.

Seating is a critical issue because it determines the number of people who can attend, and therefore, the admissions you can collect. Rental cost is also a critical issue because it is directly tied into the bottom line. We knew if we chose the Grange our audience would be smaller, but if we chose the Seaview Theater our expenses would be higher. At this point the decision rests on "the numbers" and two other intangible factors. You can run the show for an extra weekend to meet financial goals, but that puts a large obligation on the cast and crew, and is not something we would recommend for a small community. If you want high attendance for revenues, community response, and involvement, choose the larger venue, pay for it and rely on increased buzz to fill the seats next year. Finally, the cost attached to a larger auditorium may well be swallowed up by the greater seating capacity.

You can also hope for a fortuitous event as happened to us. Rosario Resort, the local resort hotel and largest employer on the island, opened a banquet and convention facility. Gil Geiser, the owner, was a community-spirited man and generous benefactor to many local causes. We sat on the front steps of the resort with him one day and told him of the vision to create a community center for the arts on Orcas Island. He offered the use of the building to us free of charge and we were able to use it for many years. He supported our goals and was willing to contribute in any way possible.

Some groups, such as those located in retirement communities, will have a built-in venue. This is a gift.

Technical Assistance

It is important to have your sound and lighting man give you the specifications needed for the show. Before you make a final decision, take him with you to check out the site. Experience in the field will enable him to spot and evaluate problems, and be able to ask specific questions of the site manager or engineer. The site engineer is an invaluable source of information. He will know electrical capacities, critical outlets, and structural limitations. If you rent a large, professional theater, there are many extra costs you may have to incur—for example, there may be union or legal issues that will make it necessary for you to pay for the services of a professional stage crew.

If you know of, or have used, a certain space, experience will save hundreds of dollars. Another possibility is to find someone in your group with connections to a theater or venue that can negotiate a reduced fee and help you understand the limitations of the building.

Checklist for Choosing a Venue

Make a list of all the items you will need to rent or borrow that the venue does not provide. Rely on your volunteer experts with experience in theater to find out about all the technical capacities of the space, including:

- Lighting
- Sound equipment including microphones
- Cords
- Power outlets
- Backstage area for props
- Size of stage
- Area for band
- Dressing for males and females
- Makeup and hairdressing area
- Costume racks
- Area for people to gather before going onstage
- Lobby or foyer
- Bathrooms for performers—and for audience!
- An area to sell products or hold raffles
- Box office
- Refreshment area

If, for some reason, you are unable to find an indoor venue, there is the possibility of renting a huge tent for your show. If you have access to a large piece of land with ample parking space, a tent can be a great solution, depending on the weather in your area. A tent can be costly, but perhaps you have a connection with someone who owns a production company that may be willing to lend a tent in exchange for acknowledgment and publicity.

If you decide on using a tent, you begin with a bare bones operation and everything has to be brought in and set up. This includes chairs, stage, decorations, sound system, lighting, adequate power source (110 and 220), piano or keyboard, choir risers, exit signs, permits from the fire marshal, sound boards, water systems, and steps for the stage. This involves a lot of time, money and effort, so proceed with caution. Over the years, Colleen supervised many large events in her church for which they rented huge tents.

Your best bet is to search until you find an indoor venue with enough seating to make your fundraiser worthwhile. How fortunate if you have your own stage setup available within your community or organization. If not, keep searching and don't overlook movie theaters, school gymnasiums, and Grange Halls. Many times, your event will have a "built in" audience if it is being produced in a church, school, or town meeting hall.

☆ Date ☆

On Orcas Island, we knew summertime was out of the question for a show. Tourism was, and still is, the biggest industry and the three months of summer in Washington State were dedicated to business and service. February, on the other hand, was the pits. Cold nights were spent huddled by the fireside and activities were at a minimum. Actually, they were virtually nonexistent.

We always chose the last two weekends in February for our performances. Some years, we only performed one weekend because that's all our participants could give as they had jobs and families to be considered. The Northwest isn't typically snow country, so February was perfect. Those who live in Chicago or other snowy areas should take weather into consideration because one bad snowstorm can obliterate the whole project.

Schedule

Our method was to begin talking about the show before Thanksgiving with the end of February as the goal date. After the first year, we knew we had a reliable cadre we could count on, wannabe's who were not included in the last show, and newcomers who we could recruit. There was no formal organization to which we answered or around which we organized. When it was time, we just got going. The organizing principal was the show itself. We looked at the calendar, selected a few dates and booked the best available at Discovery House at Rosario Resort.

We recruited some people who would fit certain characters to impersonate and the "buzz" began to generate other ideas. Individuals would approach us and say things like, "My brother and I want to sing 'I've Got You, Babe' dressed as Sonny and Cher. Would that be okay?" Generally, the answer was yes, in keeping with our inclusive philosophy. We would discuss it and if it seemed to be a fit, we would give the go-ahead, and if it didn't, we would suggest other ways they could be involved. We logged each suggestion into our notebooks and people began thinking about their parts. Christmas was on the way, so we knew we couldn't get any actual work done over the holidays, but that month was devoted to thinking, and planning.

Around January 2, we would get down to business. The writing team met, the individual acts began to rehearse, the volunteers were in place and the team leaders were working on their jobs. Since our performances were always the last weekend in February, everyone knew exactly how much time they had to get ready for dress rehearsal. This gave the cast and crew a sense of security as they were able to budget their time accordingly.

We contacted everyone who had expressed a desire to be included and began making a schedule to visit the various acts to make suggestions on costumes, staging, and musical accompaniment if needed. The beauty of a variety show as opposed to a scripted production such as *Oliver* is that acts can be rehearsed separately so people don't have to be at group rehearsals every evening for two months. This also cuts down on renting rehearsal space.

We were pretty well organized, but not as meticulously scheduled as some. Some groups set up tight production calendars with every rehearsal and performance listed so participants can stay on top of targeted dates. Phyllis Carney, who still lives of Orcas Island, directed the Lions Club Follies six years in a row. The members of the Lions Club presented their shows as fundraisers for various charitable causes. At the beginning of the production period, each member received a calendar with all dates written down. Rehearsals were held in real estate offices, classrooms at the school, and private homes.

The director was present at every rehearsal. The production calendar allowed the members to plan ahead for skit rehearsals, tech rehearsals, dress rehearsals, and the actual shows. These shows were made up entirely of skits, recitations, and occasional poetry readings, so there were no musical rehearsals involved; if music had been part of the event, musicians, music coaches, and musical rehearsals would have to be part of the mix as well.

Your variety show could easily become an annual event for your group, so a specific date that can be relied upon will make it easier for volunteers to plan vacations and family activities around it. Above all, give yourselves adequate time to prepare. The first show might take as long as a year to get everything together, whereas the notes, a good database, photographs, and other information gathered can cut preparation time down considerably for the next year.

When you choose a specific date for your show, there are several issues to take into consideration. Start with three dates in mind as you begin to search for a venue, as this will allow you more flexibility. Most cities and towns have a community calendar that lists all events and festivals planned for the year. Certainly the Chamber of Commerce has one. Look at the schedule for your organization to make sure no conflicting events are already planned. Be aware of national events or "special" days such as Super Bowl Sunday, Academy Awards, or holidays. The variety show involves a diversified group of people and what might be irrelevant to some may be important to others. Whatever you do, don't plan something in conflict with a long-standing traditional, local event. Be sensitive to the community culture.

The community calendar is also a great way to promote your show. When planning your date, be sure you check publication dates. You should also decide how many performances you want to have. One weekend? Two? Or more? Do you want to do Friday and Saturday nights only or do you want to add a Sunday matinee? We found that fewer were better. Our volunteer cast and crew had jobs, families, and other commitments to meet and were more willing to participate if they didn't have to make a long-term commitment to several shows.

The answer to the question about number of performances is so group specific that it is entirely in your hands. You have to consider availability of site, length of run, and the personal time commitments of the co-directors and volunteers.

Those who live in a senior community are generally retired and will have more time to rehearse and work on details. They will usually have large common areas in the complex that solves the venue problem. The co-directors of shows at Holiday Village in Mesa, Arizona, a fifty-five-plus community, told us it was easy to schedule events as the calendar is presented in January and they simply put their names on the dates they want. They have a huge stage and dance floor, so all rehearsals can be held on the stage with the directors supervising. They never have to leave the premises as everything is there and, in a sense, belongs to them. Anna Larson, director of shows for a fifty-five-plus community in Tempe, Arizona, also has no problem getting desired dates. Their shows are always presented in January since there are more people (snowbirds) in the park during the winter months. If you live in this sort of community, find out when the new calendar is coming out, select your dates, and put them in. Do not forget to reserve times for rehearsals as well as performances. That way, others will have to work around your schedule. Even though most acts will rehearse at their own places, you will need to have access to the venue during the final week before you open so you can set up your stage and backstage layouts, entrances and exits, deal with technical issues, and be sure everyone is oriented.

☆ Lead Time ☆

The first year you do a variety show is a new experience for your club or organization. Begin planning at least four to six months ahead. It can take more or less time depending on what you have available. For instance, a secured venue or clubhouse, a paid staff that can support you in this venture, which may include a special event planner or a fundraising director, will expedite your planning time.

A senior community planning a Broadway musical medley in its own theater or clubhouse will obviously require far less time to prepare than a revue mounted by a group of busy parents and children who have little experience with performing or with fundraising. Again, a show of this type could easily become a traditional event that you present year after year. Your show can be tied to a specific date that can be relied on, and will make it easier for volunteers to plan vacations and family activities around it.

☆ Same Time, Next Year ☆

The first year you produce your show, you will stumble around, you will make mistakes, but sweat, adrenaline, safety pins, and prayers will get you to your goal. It's very important that you keep good records as you go through this seminal experience. Keep track of what worked and who worked well together, and the pieces of the puzzle will start to fall into place. The fundraiser becomes easier each time because you have all your notes from your debriefings, your volunteers are in place, the job descriptions have been written, and you have a database of people to draw from. And don't forget the benefit that comes from the bonding experience that performing together can foster: many members from the year before will have become friends and will begin planning their acts for the coming year. And the showstoppers from this year are a natural fit for next year's spectacular.

CHAPTER 4

Publicize Your Fundraising Event

Of course people need to know what you are doing. The design of your materials, the quality of your written materials, the clarity of your mission statement, the availability of publicity outlets, the size of your budget, and the amount of community involvement will all contribute to success. Many options for publicizing your event are free, and reasonably priced advertising does exist. You need to be creative and alert to opportunities.

☆ Stories from the Stage ☆

To my mind, the biggest mistake a novice fundraiser makes is to think too rigidly when it comes to making contacts. Sure, cash-rich and successful companies in your community are great and obvious resources that should indeed be placed at the top of your solicitation list—but never underestimate the power of the grassroots little guys in your environment as well.

Community involvement, for me, has proven to be a surprisingly fruitful vein to tap. Years ago, I was producing a small, fledgling musical in Boston. We could barely afford the rent on the hot, cramped, matchbox of a space we were presenting in, couldn't pay our cast members at all, the whole catastrophe. My partners and I decided our only option was to bankroll ourselves with a fundraiser, or the show wasn't going to go forward. We were green at the time, but smart enough to know that big business contacts would probably ignore our solicitation (and with no track record, we were right). Our solution was to hold a "Seventies shampoo commercial fundraiser," as we called it—you'll remember, "you tell two friends, and they tell two friends, and so on, and so on . . ."

We asked every cast member, crew member, friend, family member, and associate we knew to tell AT LEAST two friends, about our (initially modest) little fundraiser, and ask them to tell AT LEAST two more. We decided to request the minimum sum of $20 in cash to be donated from everyone we contacted (modest-sounding, yes, but a huge help to our nonexistent cash flow). We recruited our cast members to provide entertainment (and schmoozing) in costume, and stocked up on inexpensive wine and cheese. Long story short: word-of-mouth pays off! The house we held the event at was overrun with more folks than a college keg party, and we were able to sweet-talk MANY guests into donating a lot more than $20, once they saw that the production we were presenting was high-caliber fun.

Sage advice: Make the work you're doing seem so appealing, your fundraising contacts will feel they're truly missing out if they aren't a part of it. And PROMINENTLY note your benefactors' names in your promotional materials—they absolutely love it!

—Lisa Mulcahy, theater director and author of Building the Successful Theater Company *and* Theater Festivals

☆ What We Did ☆

We had posters, flyers, a weekly paper, and bulletin boards at the laundromat and school. We papered every wall and bulletin board we could find with flyers and posters. We placed as many ads as we could afford in the local weekly paper as the date approached. Fortunately, in a town the size of Eastbound, everyone in the cast and crew was related to someone, or lived next door to neighbors who knew someone, and they all wanted to attend. Like Lisa Mulcahy's show, 90 percent of our success was simply word of mouth.

☆ What We Learned ☆

State how your fundraiser dollars are to be used. Incorporate it in your mission statement and goals. The volunteers must know what they are working for, the sponsors must know what they are contributing to, and the public wants to know why they should attend. Generalities do not cut the mustard. "Donate to the school" is not as effective as "Donate to the Collection for the School Library!" It is important that your word matters. Over the years, people must see adequate progress is being made toward the goal.

Many times in our experience someone would say, "I would have been there if only I had known when it was happening." Promote. Promote. Promote. Many avenues are available for publicity; don't spend funds unless you have a clear idea how they can bring a great return on your investment. Advertising is expensive, so look for inexpensive ways to repeat your message often through flyers, newsletters, and posters. Take advantage of radio and television public service announcements. Of course, word of mouth is the best and least expensive. Lisa Mulcahy's idea to tell two people and ask each of them to tell two more is ingenious, free, and inexpensive. Send cast members in costume to service organizations or popular gathering spots to promote the show, hand out flyers, and sell tickets. As soon as you have made a commitment to doing the show, and have a date and venue set, your publicity team should kick into full gear. Meet with the publicity team and the graphic artist. Hold a creative brainstorming session and be sure to think outside the box.

The overall image and, particularly the logo, repeats itself throughout the marketing material. Every piece should be immediately recognizable and easy to read. Marketing materials, with lots of white space, grab attention. Each time the image is seen it leaves an impression. Generally, the first time, it is just noticed. By the fourth or fifth time, it becomes an integral part of the consciousness. Some people are visual, some tactual, and some are auditory, so each form should be covered.

When considering promotion, be sure to coordinate your budget with your schedule. Start slowly and economically. Increase your budget and exposure as you approach the opening. Don't blow it all the first week. A good designer and/or marketing person can help you set up a schedule. (See appendix A for a helpful list of tips.)

☆ Marketing Materials ☆

Your marketing materials should include the following items and information:

- Logo
- Event name
- Producing organization
- Purpose, i.e., to build a community theater, or buy new uniforms

- Location
- Dates and times of performances
- Ticket prices and general and preferred seating
- Hotline phone (optional)
- Web site address (optional)
- Any other important information
- Try to leave as much white space as possible

We didn't have the benefits of the Web in our early years, but we have used electronic advertising and communications in later productions. If you have access and resources you should certainly use the medium to promote your show. You may want to contact your local phone company to set up a phone hotline. We found that a hotline required extra time, so a volunteer team of seven was organized and each volunteer was assigned to one day a week. That way, messages could be retrieved at any time during the volunteer's specified day; then she could return the phone call (today she could e-mail the answer).

The Web makes the sharing of information much easier. Each volunteer is e-mailed a document covering your publicity information and frequently asked questions. In addition to getting information, customers can order tickets through the Web site or the hotline. This is a great way to sell tickets and promote. Obviously, natural sales people or promoters love to do this.

☆ Ways to Promote ☆

The following list outlines different ways to promote your show, in ascending order of cost:

- Word of mouth
- Flyers
- Posters
- Press releases, reviews, and articles
- Community calendars—don't forget, these appear not only in newspapers but also on local radio and television stations
- Written testimonials after first show
- Chamber of Commerce bulletins, newsletters, and magazines
- Church bulletins
- Complimentary tickets
- Newspapers ads

- Hotline phone number
- Web site
- Radio
- TV

Word of Mouth

There is nothing like the power of word-of-mouth advertising. It is free and it can be the most effective activity to build interest. It spreads like wildfire and can sell out your show, as well as bind your community together.

Posters and Flyers

Posters and flyers are the easiest and least expensive way to advertise an event. They are basically the same, with the only difference being size and space allotted for display. Local bulletin boards are readily available and a small flyer will be easier to fit on the board. Some businesses will allow posters, but they are generally reluctant to relinquish a large space in their storefront windows. Libraries, doctors' offices, dentists' offices, medical centers, senior centers and restaurants often have community bulletin boards and might be happy to display these for you. In larger communities, businesses will be more willing to display your material if they are connected or somehow involved in the show. In a smaller town, there is a hometown support group that is naturally accustomed to promoting local events. Flyers can also be hand delivered or used as doorknob hangers. Cut a slit in the flyer so these will fit and not blow away. All flyers and posters need to be consistent with your other publicity material.

Press Releases and Articles in the Local Paper

Contact the entertainment editor of your local paper and ask if he or she would be willing to write an article and insert a picture to plug the show. Write your own press release and send it to the editor. Don't forget the local papers in nearby cities and towns. The press release is one of the most important and effective marketing tools you will use to promote your show. The format for writing a press release is specific. Webwire.com provides a succinct description of the parts of a press release and how to write one (*www.webwire.com/FormatGuidelines.asp*). You start with a headline—not too many words, maybe a brief sentence. This is followed by a first paragraph—"a strong, introductory paragraph that grabs the reader's attention," according to Webwire—and contains the information most relevant to your message such as the five *Ws*—who, what, when, where, and why.

Subsequent paragraphs should expand on the themes and information contained in the opening paragraph. If people involved with the event have something pithy and related to say, their quotes can be woven into the body of the release.

As Webwire continuously stresses, fact checking, proper spelling, and correct grammar are of utmost importance, because "you are writing a press release to grab the attention of the media." If you want the media to report your release as news, or to include it in listings for the public, it has to be accurate and interesting. As the Web site goes on to state, "effective releases usually utilize a strategy known as the inverted pyramid, which is written with the most important information and quotes first."

For other sites about press releases: visit *http://ga.essortment.com/advertisingbusi_rlsz.htm.*

Enclose a brief cover letter to the newspaper editor on your letterhead explaining the purpose of the release and informing her when you would like it to run.

Chamber of Commerce

Many Chambers publish full-color quarterly magazines. Think ahead and give yourself lead time so your article with pictures will appear in the issue prior to your production.

Organization Newsletters

Don't limit yourself to the sponsoring organization. Many times, people involved in the show also belong to Kiwanis, Lions, Rotary, Boys and Girls Club, Sports Boosters, and, of course, the Chamber of Commerce. Find any group with a newsletter as they are always looking for articles and pictures to promote coming attractions.

Church Bulletins

Design a catchy piece that includes all pertinent information. This is a way to disseminate information at no cost. Some churches will only include announcements under the auspices of their group, whereas others are likely to accept news from outside organizations if the promoters are parishioners or they deem the project beneficial to the community.

☆ Written and Video Testimonials ☆

If this is your first show, get written and/or video testimonials from cast members who will write or speak about what this experience means to them through their gift of service. They can share information about the fundraiser, and their personal enthusiasm about being in an organization that taps into their creativity. These testimonials can be used on your Web site, TV, radio, newspapers, and all promotional material.

For example, here's what Mike Schifsky, an original cast member of "Orcas Tonight," had to say: "I'm not sure how I got talked into being 'Bowser' in Colleen and Gail's variety show. Especially not sure how I came to wear a gold lamé costume in front of three hundred people, and then have the nerve to actually try to sing.

"Colleen and Gail hatched the idea of a Variety Show to raise money for a proposed community theater. A noble goal. However, the notion took on a life of its own. There was a loose-knit group of friends on Orcas who frequented events like the annual Family Festival or the Fireman's Ball. The perpetrators of the Variety Show idea enlisted many of these friends to participate. The whole thing sort of snowballed.

"The girls came up with the idea of a take-off on the singing group Sha Na Na. Somehow I got roped into being Bowser. Maybe because I could sing a little, maybe because I'm skinny. I balked at the gold lamé, but it did me little good.

"We practiced and practiced until we had 'Barbara Anne' and 'Runaround Sue' down pat. The rehearsals were great fun, but eventually the day of reckoning came, and we had to face an actual audience. I remember the stage fright, and the sure fact that I was going to make an ass of myself. When our group was onstage, and the lights came up. I felt totally alone. Then someone on the piano hit the first note of 'Barbara Anne.' I caught it and started belting the song. Everyone else in the group came in on cue, and we breezed through it just like rehearsal. Even Schmitter. Next came 'Runaround Sue.' Mary Lou came bopping onstage in her poodle skirt and wowed the audience. We were on a roll. After that it was a breeze. Instead of dreading each performance, I could hardly wait."

Radio

Local radio stations will often donate airtime or give you an on-air interview. In some places, short radio spots are available if you purchase a certain amount of spots for a limited number of days on a special promotion. Check with local stations and they might offer free time or give you a price break because it is a fundraiser.

Television

A great way to call attention to your fundraiser is to appear on local early morning shows that are always looking for community interest stories. Television commercials are expensive, but there are ways to circumvent this challenge. It never hurts to ask and the unexpected shows up again and again.

Don't be bashful about calling your local television station, and be prepared for the unexpected. For example, Colleen's daughters Shannon and Michele wrote to KOMO TV Channel 4 in Seattle, Washington, saying that their Mom and teacher were producing a show on Orcas Island, Washington, called "Orcas Tonight."

Shannon and Michele invited the station to come to Orcas Island and do a story about the event. You can imagine our excitement when the girls received a letter from *PM Northwest* that they loved the idea, and they would be coming up to film parts of the show. It didn't take long for the news to spread and create a publicity buzz. The "Orcas Tonight" show feature aired three weeks later and the cast and crew were invited to Norm and Mary Ann Carpenter's home for a potluck and viewing of the *PM Northwest* show.

The segment opened up with the *PM Northwest* film crew on the ferry as it approached Orcas Island. It was a wonderful shot with the island in the distance, as the ferry approached the dock. They filmed people preparing for the show, guests arriving and segments of the show itself. This creative idea was birthed from two children, so don't underestimate the places where creativity will show up.

Web Site

This is a place to search out someone who is willing to donate the time to create a Web site or negotiate a low fee, as this can be a time-consuming endeavor. A Web site can be created with a simple one page promotion and pertinent information.

Your Program

As the graphic designer is creating the publicity material for the event, he or she is thinking ahead to the design elements of the program presented to the audience upon arrival at the show. Of course, all visual materials need to portray the same image. Remember that your program will travel out the door in many pockets and purses. At that time, the program becomes a marketing piece as it is shared, sparking interest of others.

☆ Ticket Sales ☆

Some places to sell tickets from are obvious: local businesses, through board members of your organization, and online from your Web site. Many people like to have online ticket sales available. Of course, selling tickets online means that you will have to figure out how you are going to implement such sales. Are you going to accept reservations via e-mail and let the buyers do the actual paying when they arrive at the theater? Does your organization have a system in place through which patrons can make online purchases using their credit cards? You could also have a tickets phone hotline, but you would still have to consider the same issues (reservations only, or can you make the actual sale, through credit card information, over the phone?)

Handing out a packet of tickets to cast and crew members is not advisable as it is too difficult to keep track of these sales. And it is important that you do keep track of all sales. If you are selling tickets in a group that sells tickets on an ongoing basis such as a church, you will have a ticket sale table, or box office, located in the lobby.

CHAPTER 5

······························

Creating a Top-Notch Program

The printed program is the first thing your audience will see as they walk through the door. The program makes a statement about the quality of the show and the organization. It is also a fundamental guide and information source to the events of the next two hours. It can be simple or elaborate depending on time, dollars, and donated expertise.

☆ Stories from the Stage ☆

I remember the time I was stressed and hadn't given myself enough lead-time to complete everything that needed to be done. When the graphic arts designer presented me with the completed program for the show, I looked at it quickly and said, "Fine. Print it." Unfortunately, four names of the cast members had been misspelled. The programs had to be re-printed the day before opening night. I learned a hard lesson. Always take the time to check and re-check all printed materials before signing off!

—Bonnie Fairchild, event coordinator, Atlanta, Georgia

☆ What We Did ☆

Our first program was a simple 8 1/2" × 11" paper, folded over to give us four pages. We made a clever cover and crammed as much information as we could include about the show and all the people who had helped us. We proofed the information, proofed it again, and were careful not to leave out someone's name, or misspell a word.

We used a copier at the school to print our programs. Paper and ink were donated to the cause. Today you can design a great looking program on the computer using ready-made templates, print all the copies on a home copier, or make copies at a local quick-print shop like Kinko's.

☆ What We Learned ☆

The first choice is to find a professional designer who is willing to donate his or her services. We recommend you use the same designers for all visual material as this creates consistency in your design elements and builds up image recognition throughout your campaign. It is important to include the graphic designer from the very beginning. The designer will be inspired and capture the essence of the show by being a part of the core team. If your organization is a nonprofit, or operates under the auspices of a legitimate nonprofit corporation, it might not be that difficult to get a design firm to donate its services. Designers are often very interested in using their well-polished communication skills to promote social good. Of course, nowadays, myriad software and templates are available for the design of all kinds of presentational materials—everything from posters to programs. If you don't have a professional designer, you certainly have someone who is an expert at assembling and generating a templated design.

By this time, you have a logo that can be used on the cover of the program, but you need to develop an image representative of the show to be used on the program, posters, and flyers. It should be simple and portray an image representing a highlight of the show. We used drawings on our covers of the featured acts. An Al Jolson silhouette was extremely effective. The high school art teacher designed the image and we repeated it on posters, flyers, newspaper ads, and the programs.

Choosing high quality materials reflects the quality of your commitment to success. Find a stationery vendor or paper distributor and printer willing to donate or provide services at cost in exchange for publicity or acknowledgment on the program itself. Your designer will help you. (See appendix A for a helpful list of tips.)

☆ Suggested Program Contents ☆

Your front cover should include:

- Image—a scene from the show or a sketch
- Title
- Location

- Date and time
- Organization

The inside pages and back cover should include:

- Goals
- Acts or scenes
- Intermission
- Volunteers
- Special thanks and recognition to large donors or those otherwise not recognized

You have the option to list volunteers by category or by name. If you plan to list names of all volunteers, appoint one person whose task it is to produce a list of volunteer positions and names. Enter the names into a database and it can be directly e-mailed to two or three people to review position, names, and correct spelling before it is sent to the designer. Be sure to list all participants and acts. Use one or two pages depending on volume of material. Include musicians, lighting, choreographers, prop person, writers, and stage crew. If you plan to print names of volunteers, don't leave anyone out. This causes hurt feelings and you are probably better off to give a blanket "Thank You" to all volunteers.

You can include ads in your program, but you need to decide if the added complications and costs outweigh the benefits. Check with your designer and printer. It is much easier to produce a program created from an 8 1/2" × 11" sheet folded once, which yields a four-page conventional document. Space is limited and virtually no space can be dedicated to advertising. It is a cheap, simple format, and recommended for novices like we were. As you grow and want to expand the dimensions or number of pages, you must consider cost of paper, folding, stapling, risk of errors and typos (yes, all these processes cost money) versus price of ad space, selling ads, and total income. Obviously, most organizations opt for a larger, slick format with ad space, because they can bring in extra income. Also, the companies that advertise are committing more than their dollars to your project. They are saying, in effect, "We support this cause and these people." Graphic designers deal with all these variables on a day-to-day basis and you should consult with them to determine the best way to proceed.

If you include ads, they should be supplied by the businesses that buy them. A simple way to do this is to ask for a business card from the company. The heading could read: "Supporters of Cottonwood School," then put in as many cards as you have room to include. The businesses could pay a hundred dollars each to be included; obviously you will adjust the cost of the ads to what the traffic will bear. Make sure that you proofread everything with extreme care. We tried including ads once and it turned out to be more trouble than it was worth in terms of time spent to make everything come out just right.

CHAPTER 6

·······························

Budget for Production

By the time we had a second show, we realized we better get more organized and have a budget, and not expect cast, crew, and community to continue to fund the entire show without some outside resources. We made a list of things we knew would be needed and that became our operating budget. Over the years, the budget, record keeping, awareness of royalties, the importance of insurance, and the hidden expenses became more and more evident. Although we continued to operate on donated time and money, we knew we had to be prepared to find funds for the show.

☆ Stories from the Stage ☆

I had a meeting with all volunteers to caution them about overspending. I announced that each act had fifteen dollars allocated for costumes, so it would be advisable to use found items from their closets or go to the local consignment store.

Four young ladies seated in the back row were chatting away during my little speech. They left the meeting enthusiastically talking about their costumes, the best colors to choose and appropriate accessories to make them look magnificent. Imagine my surprise when the receipts were turned in and each member of the act had rented elaborate costumes for fifty dollars each instead of the fifteen dollars designated for each act! They had heard "fifty" instead of "fifteen." Luckily, it didn't completely break the bank and they did, indeed, look spectacular!

—George Sanderson, CPA, Pensacola, Florida

✶ What We Did ✶

Budget?!?! What budget? Are you kidding? We wanted to do a show, raise some money for our Center for the Arts, so we just started and let the money take care of itself. Back in the early eighties, we knew we didn't have access to corporate sponsors (there were no corporations on the island), but we were in such a tight-knit community. Most of our participants were middle-income people who couldn't afford large donations, but wanted to be involved in a grassroots venture that would be fun and help raise money for the proposed center. We simply asked all people involved if they would be willing to pay for their own costumes, makeup, wigs, and accessories. Everyone agreed to this arrangement and it was clear from the start that we had no nest egg from which to draw. Everyone involved was a volunteer.

We gave no thought as to how we were going to pay for the show. We just knew we wanted to do it and figured everything would fall into place. It was like an old Andy Hardy movie where Mickey Rooney says, "Hey, I have an idea! Let's put on a show!" Then Judy Garland says, "I know where there's an old barn!" and they were off and running. They certainly didn't prepare a budget or have any idea what they were going to do; they just did it.

When we had expenses, we dug into our own pockets, went to Russ at the local hardware store, or Kay at the consignment shop, explained the project, and asked if we could charge lumber, electrical cords, capes, vintage dresses, or whatever was needed. We promised to pay them back when the ticket sale proceeds were counted. Not one person turned us down, so we were able to operate on the proverbial shoestring.

✶ What We Learned ✶

A good budget will keep everyone on track and ensure the profits go where they're intended. A starting budget should be one of the first items set in place. It will provide a guideline for projected expenses, and help you begin certain projects like venue rental and publicity. We began our first show with zero assets, but in the following years, we knew we could get cash out of the account established from the previous year's performance if we needed to do so. As is often the case, the shows became more expensive as everyone wanted to top the previous performances with more intricate sets, costumes, and effects. It, therefore, became necessary to keep track of the budget.

We set up our budget by guesstimating how much we had spent the previous year in each category (costumes, rentals, printing, etc.). Once you start to keep track of your budget, you no longer have to guesstimate these figures; they should be part of your records. If we knew that we wanted to do something more expensive the next year than we had the previous—rent or purchase better microphones, perhaps—we "projected" a higher level of expenditure in that area. Recruit a good bookkeeper or accountant to get you started off right.

Go to pages 172–173 to see what our simple operating budget sheet looked like. You won't find categories for the silent auction, raffles, and sponsors, as they were not part of the budget for our original island shows. These came later when Colleen was the event planner for a large church in Oregon. Your organization may be more or less sophisticated and you can change this to suit your specific needs.

Note that in order for the actual expenditures to be calculated, lots of receipts will need to be saved and logged in, and a running budget that itemizes each individual expense will need to be maintained.

If your performance is taking place under the aegis of an established nonprofit, there may be someone in place who will help you with your bookkeeping. Otherwise you can find a volunteer with the proper expertise. Nowadays, nearly everyone has a computer, and nearly all come with some sort of spreadsheet or rudimentary table program, so you can probably maintain the books yourself in a pinch.

☆ Keeping Track ☆

Your budget should be one of the first things to be considered and set in place. An accountant or bookkeeper can help list the funds available for seed money and any contributions from sponsors or donors. List and track all expenses starting with venue rental. Add about 20 percent to all line items in case you go over. Have the financial director keep track of all expenditures by keeping in close contact with each team leader and encourage anyone who needs to purchase something to go to their team leader with the request. The team leader keeps all receipts and hands them over to the financial director. After the show, have the financial director prepare a report on all expenses and have this information available for anyone who wishes to see it.

Find out how much money was made from the show as soon as possible as cast, crew, and the public like to know the answer to the question, "How much money did we make?"

CHAPTER 7

Attorneys, Accountants, and Agents

Most theater problems we have discussed so far are apparent and easy to solve. Choosing a venue and selecting dates will be dictated by your location, budget, and other individual circumstances. However, many issues you need to deal with, though just as important, are not as evident. They include items like insurance, royalties, fire and occupancy codes, and tracking ticket sales.

☆ Stories from the Stage ☆

We received the following note from Chandler Center for the Arts. It represents a thorough and extremely wise collaboration between three municipal entities that recognize the value of theater, owning a multi-use venue available to all three:

Chandler Center for the Arts is jointly owned by the City of Chandler and the Chandler Unified School District. As such, operating costs for maintenance and some salaries are shared between the two entities. The school district has priority usage of the Center Mondays through Thursdays, which consists primarily of school-related arts activities, such as band, choir, drama, and dance. The City has priority Fridays through Sundays, and generally uses the space for public performances and rentals. The City contracts with the Chandler Cultural Foundation, a nonprofit corporation, to contract the performances and rentals.

—Katrina Mueller, director, Chandler Center for the Arts,
Chandler, Arizona

☆ What We Did ☆

When we first started raising funds for an arts center, we had a "noble cause" and figured whatever we did was okay. We didn't have a computer system that generated tickets; we didn't even buy numbered tickets because they cost too much. We literally used muffin tins for change, coffee cans for currency, and added up the take at the end of the night to see how much we had made. The last night of the run, if we had done well, we might use $100 from the take to treat the cast and crew to a round of refreshments to reward them for all the work they had done.

The next day, we took the money to Velma, a local parent, information source, coffee shop owner, and school-community booster. She was president of the Orcas (School) Booster Club, and kept all building funds in that account separate from normal operations. Velma would deposit the money in a local bank account she had, safe as Fort Knox, and hard to get as a refund from the IRS. The next year we repeated the process. The funds were always safe, and when we needed money to buy equipment or material for costumes, it was available. But, the times they were a' changin'.

☆ What We Learned ☆

Notice, in the excerpt on page 54, the Chandler Center for the Arts has a school district, a city agency, and a nonprofit corporation involved in the operation. This seems to be a win-win, enlightened agreement between three forward-looking organizations that understand the value of art, theater, and business. They share the commitment, investment, and profit of that vision, and the whole city and surrounding areas, benefit. The relationship has been maintained and profited the community over the past fifteen years.

The first warning signals that we were going to have to change our approach came with growing success. When we started in the new convention hall at Rosario Resort, and the audiences grew to overflowing, the volunteer fire chief visited one night to be sure we didn't exceed occupancy regulations. Somebody else mentioned we should think about royalties, and a tourist at the resort asked if tickets were tax deductible. Well, we assured the fire chief we would not exceed the seating limit, we hadn't thought about "royalties," and had given no consideration to setting up a legal structure that would allow patrons to claim their payments as "tax deductible."

Insurance, deductibles, and royalties had been the farthest things from our minds, but we soon saw that the money we were collecting called for a more business-like approach. In this section we present some general issues you need to consider, and direct you to the people and agencies that can give you the answers.

☆ Whom to Contact and What to Do ☆

First, we cannot provide you with all the answers because, as we have learned through experience and research, every production is different. Each state, city, and community has unique regulations, and organizations have different legal or corporate structures.

Don't panic. The answer is simple. Contact the right people in your community and ask the right questions. Seek out the people who are sympathetic to your cause and ask them to donate time, at least for a basic consultation. Network with members of local service clubs. Make a presentation at the local Lions lunch. Look for people who work in professional offices who may be able to help. The professionals will know what questions to ask. Contact a CPA or a good accountant, an insurance agent, and an attorney. Get them to help you build a secure legal/financial structure, and consult with them when new questions or new situations arise. For example, after a couple of successful years, you might decide to change your corporate structure, add an auction, or raffle an expensive prize to increase earnings. Check with your legal team, search the state Web site for applicable rules and regulations and decide if you want to proceed. Of course you will be checking with your bookkeeper and accountant on all events.

When you begin, most of your volunteers and helpers will be far more interested in doing production and making the curtain go up. Some, however, will be detail people and enjoy the "bean counter" aspects of tracking, accounting, and recording, or may even be practicing professionals who will volunteer their services for a worthy cause. Find them and use their talents. They may never sing a song or dance a jig, but the services they provide will make your life much easier. If you go the distance, and actually incorporate and become a nonprofit that accepts tax-deductible donations, you will need to have a board. Often these people will end up serving on your board and continuing to provide pro bono services.

☆ Where Are You and How Do You Proceed? ☆

If you are already operating within a school, or for an established booster group, church organization, city group working with the Chamber of Commerce, or are under the auspices of a YMCA or Boys' and Girls' Club, many of your legal concerns are probably solved. However, you must check with them to assure your project meets their policies and obligations. Meet with the organization to determine that you are covered for the protection to secure your efforts. As a CPA friend in Chandler, Arizona said, "If you are volunteering for a charitable fundraiser, don't put yourself, or your group, at risk. It doesn't make sense."

However, if you do not have the protection provided by an established organization, you can search for one in your community. Groups like the American Legion, Veterans of Foreign Wars, Soroptimists, and Knights of Columbus are eager to sponsor community programs. They will have people in their administration, or on the board, who will be able to help. You can reach these groups through personal connections or through the Chamber of Commerce.

Most of you will want to establish a relationship as described above and move toward independence, as you grow large enough to have enough history and success to feel secure. Of course, you can always start from scratch, in which case, keep on reading.

☆ Accounting ☆

Start with a good accountant or CPA. He or she can advise you on the best way to set up a nonprofit or charitable organization, and refer you to a good attorney. Tracking money is probably one of the most critical activities to the leader of any organization, but often one of the most onerous. It seems irrelevant in the excitement of starting, but is always important in the final evaluation. Find a good bookkeeper! He or she will help you prepare your budget, and keep you within it. The budget may not be exact down to the last penny, but will provide guidelines for you to follow as you move toward final production. It will also remind you of the ultimate goal and how much money you want to make from this project. If you must deviate, you will know why, and be prepared for the consequences. You don't want to be as fiscally naïve as a producer we know, who said, upon being informed that there was a monetary crisis: "We must still have money. We still have checks in the checkbook!"

Here are some of the responsibilities that can be taken care of by a good accountant and attorney working together:

- Create and maintain the corporate structure and tax status
- Make recommendations on insurance and potential liabilities in conjunction with an insurance agent
- Pay royalties

- Handle cash and tickets (sounds minor, but very important)—your accountant can help set up the system and a bookkeeper can maintain it
- Review contracts with your attorney (if applicable)
- Provide a financial history for planning the next project

✩ Legal ✩

An attorney can set up your basic legal identity and help you make tax and other essential decisions. Are you a school, city (municipal), or church organization? Are you a charity? Are you a nonprofit 501(c)(3) corporation or do you operate under the auspices of one? (Maybe so!) If you are just starting, your attorney will explain the differences, the consequences of each choice, and how to get started down the right path. When these decisions are made, your accountant can advise you on taxes, income, and donations . . . in short, the money. Every operating agreement will be different and should be agreed upon between you and your accountant or attorney.

The importance of the legal structure is that it defines the universe of law, custom, and operations within which you must operate. Once the structure is in place, and you become familiar with the rules of the game, you can deal with the business of tracking effectiveness, establishing a history you can use for the future, and, most important, protecting the integrity of all performances, productions, and general operations including income and profit.

✩ Insurance ✩

You must insure against risk and liability. Particularly if you are volunteers! When you are involved with an established organization such as a school or charitable group, most of the insurance liability will fall under their policies and reflect their history. You may want to pay for a special rider on their policy or yours. However, no matter how many Hold Harmless agreements you have, or assurances from an independent venue, you are responsible for your own negligence. As Joel Wirth, CPA, from Chandler, Arizona, says: *If you are negligent, you pay*!

The best thing to do is get a certificate of insurance or extended coverage on an existing policy. If you are independent volunteers "doing your own thing," don't risk your labor, your goals, and your own altruistic dedication to the possibility of a freak accident or miscalculation. Check with your insurance agent and the venue you are using.

☆ Royalties ☆

For beginners, royalties are often the most neglected, and one of the important, responsibilities you have as the producer of a show. When we began doing our shows, we were unaware of licensing rights or that we needed to get permission to perform certain songs. We thought a variety show for a noble cause was enough! Several years later, we became aware of licensing issues. As we became more savvy, involved people with more theater experience, and involved ourselves in the administrative operations, we realized we were violating rules and regulations, more important, depriving artists from the rightful profit from their creations. As co-directors we took on that responsibility of researching licenses and royalties, and would not use music without a careful review of the rules.

Royalties are the fees due the composer of material used in your show. The main organizations you have to deal with are ASCAP, BMI, and SESAC, organizations that act as clearinghouses for licensing music. It would be really difficult for individual composers to stay on top of all the different uses of their music: in elevators, on TV commercials, in concerts, in talent shows, etc., so that's why these large organizations handle it. However, this gets a little tricky, which is why we went to the ASCAP Web site and searched through the FAQs and other posted information in order to help us understand the issues a little more clearly.

First of all, ASCAP, BMI, and SESAC license concert or non-dramatic performances of music. The right to dramatic, or "grand rights," performances must be obtained directly from the owner of the rights—the publisher and the composer. Whether your variety show format is dramatic or non-dramatic is open to interpretation. ASCAP, in its Concert & Recital Licenses bulletin, says "In general, the perform-ance of music as part of a musical comedy opera, play with music, revue, or ballet presented in its entirety is considered to be dramatic, as would the performance of one or more musical selections from such a musical or opera accompanied by dialogue, pantomime, dance, or stage action. Rights to present dramatic performances are obtained directly from the copyright owners."

So, if your performers are wearing costumes, or acting, or doing choreography, while they sing "Easy Street," but they aren't doing the entire score of *Annie*, is it a dramatic or a non-dramatic usage? ASCAP won't make that determination, and neither will the other organizations. You will have to go directly to the publisher of the music to find out how your performance will be treated. In fact, if you are planning to include numbers from several different composers and publishers, you will have to contact each one of them. We found out that ASCAP itself presents a variety show each year, and the organizers–all members or administrators of ASCAP themselves– have to go to each publisher in order to obtain permission to use music in that context.

But wait, what if you have 501(c)(e) status or are sanctioned by a nonprofit organization? Again quoting from the ASCAP bulletin "Copyright law exempts public performances of copyrighted musical compositions . . . if all three of the following conditions are met: 1) there is no purpose of direct or indirect commercial advantage; 2) there is no payment for the performance to the performers, promoters, or organizers; and 3) if there is an admission charge, the net proceeds are used exclusively for educational, religious, or charitable purposes."

Maybe you're okay, right? But the brochure goes on to say, "In cases where there is an admission charge, however, under the statute copyright owners may nevertheless serve a notice of objection to the performance, which negates the exemption." Which really means that you may have to contact the copyright owners. It's probably best to talk to an ASCAP representative.

ASCAP's Web site has a feature called ACE Title Search. You can do a search for "Easy Street" (and the rest of your selections) and find out who composed the song, and how to contact the publisher.

Of course, if you are working for an official nonprofit with an administration and a board, you probably want to turn this job over to someone who has worked with rights and licenses in the past. And, if you personally know a composer, or know someone who knows someone and can secure rights in that manner, that, too, will work.

The sites for these organizations are *www.ASCAP.com, www.BMI.com*, and *www.SESAC.com*.

If you are interested in music in the public domain you can contact *www.pdinfo.com*. This Web site provides great information on copyright, law, and links to public domain music lists.

If you are using dramatic material in your revue or show, you're going to need to seek permission from the publisher of that work. Some of the organizations that license play productions are Samuel French, Inc. (*www.samuelfrench.com*), Baker's Plays (*www.bakersplays.com*), and

Dramatists Play Service (*www.dramatists.com*). Musical Theater International (*www.mtishows.com*) and R&H Theatricals (*www.rnh.com*) are for musicals.

☆ Raffles and Auctions ☆

Many groups are combining dinner theater with fundraising. If you wish to include raffles or auctions in your program, check the Web site for your particular state to determine operating rules and regulations.

☆ Employees ☆

Your show is probably a labor of love, as it was for us, that does not sustain anyone's livelihood. However, organizations that have their own facility, such as the Chandler Center for the Arts, are likely to have a small group of full-time employees. And even groups that rent a hall seasonally may find themselves contracting actors or musicians as special guest artists. If you have employees, you are going to have to find out about, and comply with, state and local employment laws and regulations.

CHAPTER 8

Musicians

When planning a variety show, music and musicians are of the utmost importance. We started by asking the lead member of the band that performed at the local resort if he would be interested in participating in the show. He and the lead singer agreed to ask the other band members if they would join in. They were delighted to be the "Orcas Tonight Musicians." The lead singer opened the show with a personalized song welcoming the audience and the group provided accompaniment for several acts.

☆ Stories from the Stage ☆

Hours and hours of time and energy had gone into this performance. The director had given careful consideration to developing a relationship among the crew and the players. Some criticized the effort but continued through rehearsals. The night before the performance seemed more hectic than usual.

Sound check finally ended late in the evening and we all had a sense that we might be able to pull it off Easter morning. The production cruised through the first two services with no problems. However, the third service on Easter Sunday was by far the most important of the year for this church. It had the highest attendance and supported our good works.

The service began. I came onstage and grabbed the microphone in front of 1,000 congregants. At that instant, a clap of thunder sounded, and in a moment, all was dark, not a sound to be heard. The power had gone out, and in a flash, only the murmuring congregation could be heard.

Someone whispered that we could do the song acoustically. Immediately, the drummer started the beat. In my Phys Ed teacher voice I said that the power had gone out, but not the power of our own choice to come together and create a sacred moment. I swear as I blurted out the word "power," the lights and sound came on with a RUSH. The drum-beat thundered through the room and the musicians simply bent down and plugged in their instruments without missing a note. That day the song, "The Power of One" by Johnny Clegg, took on new meaning in the lives of everyone in that room.

—Rick Brandeburg, musician and teacher, Portland, Oregon

☆ Another Story from the Stage ☆

This story is another one of ours. We called our friend Eric Funk, with whom we has worked on the "Orcas Tonight" show, for a story. He reminded us about the time when Gail was producing a fourth grade play of Beauty and the Beast *in the Seattle area, and we were absolutely stumped for music. We wanted a tape without vocals so our students could sing backed up only by music. The tape we found was from Disney, and every song had vocals. (You can now purchase CDs with orchestra only for school produc-tions.) A local pianist said she would accompany our kids, but needed four weeks to practice and rehearse, and we had only four weeks to mount the play.*

Eric was a classical musician as well as a professional pop musician who could "just play." He had left the Island to go to the Portland Symphony and then moved on to lead the Bozeman Symphony.

We called him and explained our problem.

He said, "Send me the tape and I'll play it on the piano for you and send the recording."

We said, "Great, but what about the right key and tempo and all that stuff for the kids? What if it doesn't work? And what about Disney?"

Eric said, "Don't worry, Gail, I know what they need and I will clear any rights or royalties for you with Disney or ASCAP."

We sent the tape. He recorded the music, and had it back to us in four days. We used it and it was perfect.

☆ What We Did ☆

We were fortunate because we were in a small, but desirable, location that attracted lots of gifted people. Many were not professional, but had lots of talent. We used what was available, and mostly it was good.

At times, we had to get on the ferry, drive to Seattle, and go to vintage music stores to find vinyl records, old LPs, or sheet music. We used taped music, if we could find it, but creating a tape master, running the playback machine, and cueing the music with precision is a long, difficult job. However, with new technology many of these problems can be solved using CD players and playback systems. On occasion, a volunteer pianist would step forward and offer to help. However, even one with professional experience may not have the flexibility to transpose music on the fly or play by ear. When you find such people, keep them. Such musicians are as valuable as gold. You want someone who can follow along with amateur singers who need a supportive person to give them confidence. The pianist can suggest a higher or lower range, give tips on voice control and liven up the act with some extra zings and runs. Amateurs and professionals who "just play" are the best.

☆ What We Learned ☆

It is a good idea to have a musical director. Music and musicians can present a challenge because every group and act presents different needs, which have to be delivered in such diverse ways, and every band comes with different skills and a different background. Some acts will bring their own accompaniment. Others will not. One may want a karaoke machine, and many will have no idea what to do.

☆ The Musical Director and Your Musicians ☆

The musical director is accountable for choosing the core band and other requested accompaniment for individual acts. Someone on the team researches royalties for each musical selection and follows up accordingly. Occasionally, musical charts need to be written, sheet music must be located, rehearsals must be scheduled and directed and a piano might need to be borrowed or rented. Some acts may require vocal or musical coaching assistance. The musical director or a member of the team could do this. The music brings everything to life, so the musical director has to be involved from the outset.

Our musical director was a professional musician. He spent three to four hours rehearsing with each act that wanted his help. Only a few acts needed his expertise, as the others used tapes or enlisted their own combos to accompany them. He was on hand for rehearsals and totally involved in the dress rehearsal to ensure the overall quality of the show. Even those who were left to their own devices until dress rehearsal took and implemented suggestions he made to improve their acts.

Musicians share a kind of network, have played in various bands, and usually keep contact with each other. By using this community network, you are more likely to get a higher-quality group of players faster than if you hold tryouts.

Of course, when acts have their own pianist or small combo, it reduces the responsibility of the music director and cuts down on her need to participate in ongoing rehearsals. If you are lucky enough to have a "house band," provide a list of music from the show complete with musical charts and audio CDs for each musician and singer involved. This allows the players to become familiar with the music on their own time. Don't make the players search for charts, have to figure out chord patterns, or chase down CDs on their own time. Word will spread quickly about how organized the co-directors are and that can make or break future shows.

☆ Original Music ☆

One advantage of having your own combo and pianist is their ability to write and perform original songs. Instead of using a piece of music that is copyrighted and requires royalties, original music is free for the asking and musicians love the challenge and the freedom. The great thing about original songs and parodies is that they can be personalized to speak to your community's peccadilloes. In the late seventies—and we know we're dating ourselves—Paul Simon had a popular, bittersweet song called "Fifty Ways to Leave Your Lover." In a variety revue at a small college a young man strummed the guitar as he soulfully sang a song he called "Fifty Ways to Steal a Sandwich." Since the student body was always sneaking food out of the cafeteria, this ditty was greeted with knowing guffaws.

☆ Running Musical Rehearsals ☆

The co-directors and the music director ran our dress rehearsals. We all made suggestions for changes when needed and the stage manager was always on-hand to time each act so we knew how long the show would run. Here are some tips we learned that will help you have a painless rehearsal process. The singers and musicians need to be motivated and praised. They give time and talent, and should be told they are appreciated for doing so. Rehearsals should be disciplined, tight, and organized. If there are multiple characters in the show, schedule specific times for people to show up and rehearse. The onstage performers only rehearse their own numbers, but the band has to work with them all. Stay as true to that time schedule as you can. Participants will appreciate your concern for their time and will give you an even greater effort because of the respect you show.

People who are more professional will show up and move skillfully through their parts, which in turn gives you more time to direct the people who need more attention. This kind of show is an extension of the relationships formed in the making and creation of it, so encourage personal connection. Stay open to the creativity of the group you have assembled. Don't get caught up in the narrowness of your own vision. The people involved can bring a dynamic and a creativity that can flourish in a supportive environment. This is especially true in community-based productions.

☆ Use Your Computer! ☆

Finding the perfect music for each act can be time-consuming and take considerable research. The Internet is an incredible help in locating old songs. Once, we typed in five words of a one-hundred-year-old song and in two minutes we had all the words, plus variant renditions, and a live musical version—all for the downloading!

CHAPTER 9

....

Construction, Lighting, and Sound

inding the people who can build sets, connect wires, and set up lights and sound is critical to a smoothly run show and final success. Of course many professional stage technicians exist, however, you may have to work with local mechanics who have limited stage experience. You will be amazed at how quickly they adapt their knowledge to your particular problems. So often we would tell a local technician what we needed, and the problem would be solved in no time.

☆ Stories from the Stage ☆

*The word "perfect" in the title of my book (*The Perfect Stage Crew*) is an ironic joke, but some people don't get it. You hear it a lot backstage whenever something goes wrong . . . "Perfect!" Sometimes you'll hear, "Perfect, just perfect." It's a sort of "Woe is me" exclamation used when the crew can't cuss.*

In my thirteen years of teaching at Blair High School, in Silver Spring, Maryland, I let my kids do all the work. After all, they're the ones in school. I make it a point of pride to vacate backstage just before the opening curtain and let them run the show until the bows conclude. I've only had to break that rule once:

We were doing West Side Story, *and had spent an enormous amount of time and effort on the fire escape scene. You only see the fire escape once, but we felt it was important for it to look really real, with practical windows and an authentic fire escape ladder.*

The crew put in hours of overtime and we ended up with a sixteen-foot tall, sixteen-foot wide, eight-foot deep monstrosity that looked great. In order to cantilever the fire escape out from the set we added huge braces from behind, and put hundreds of pounds of stage weights on the upstage side so it wouldn't topple.

My director and I had seen the traveling revival and when Tony climbed the fire escape the entire construction almost toppled. I wasn't having any of that so we redoubled everything for strength. Maria had an upstage escape, so she could actually climb out the window, Tony had an authentic-looking fire-escape ladder to climb, and a trash can to hop up on. The windows had curtains, we even hung extra light pipes so we could spot their love song. It was pretty impressive. And of course it was all on wheels, and had to roll on and off in a blackout.

Everything went fine through dress rehearsal, and opening night was terrific. In spite of the blackout the audience could see the stage crew rolling the unit off, and it was the only place in the show where the crew could be seen. So I instructed them to stay behind, upstage of the unit, when they pushed it off. Oops. That tiny little change meant this huge unit didn't run straight any longer, and, sure enough, it caught on the act curtain the next night. "Perfect." I figured the crew could clear it but the curtain fouled in the metal fire escape and the entire unit was stuck in place.

I waited as long as I could stand it. I rushed backstage, in the black-out, then moved onstage, and tore the curtain free. We all pushed the unit onstage again, gave it a superhuman upstage shove, and it finally rolled into its proper place. By this time the sell-out crowd had adjusted their eyes to the dim light. Everyone was watching the drama-within-a-drama unfold, including the actors.

When the unit was off I was left alone onstage, and that's when the applause started. I considered taking a bow, thought it would not be dignified, and scooted offstage as quickly as I could. The show was great, the audience was forgiving, and I finally got to be onstage. Plus, the audience could not see the eleven-foot long tear in the act curtain. Perfect, just perfect.

—John Kaluta, technical director and author of
The Perfect Stage Crew

☆ Another Story from the Stage ☆

The cast was onstage in the middle of a Carol Burnett skit when all of a sudden the electricity in the whole place went off. No one onstage knew what to do. The backstage crew was flipping switches when suddenly, our

"Harvey Corman," in a grand old stage tradition, leaped into the breach, and said in a loud stage voice, "Mama, I TOLD you to pay the power bill before we started all of this!" Meanwhile, backstage, our jack-of-all-trades electrician—God bless him!—found and flipped the master circuit breaker. The lights came on, and the show continued without missing a beat. Well, maybe we missed a beat, but we added a good laugh and another emergency was solved. Get good people!

—Carol Foster, backstage crew, Eastsound, Washington

☆ What We Did ☆

We were lucky in many operations with our first productions, but one of the most fortunate was the "mechanics." We had many builders, electricians, and all-around handymen on the island. Guys who could fix anything from a toaster to a D-8 Caterpillar. If we needed a set built, a light installed, or a special connector for speakers, someone would do it, find it or figure out a way to get it done. We told them what we needed and they did it. Many of these people were the ones we recruited out of the local hangout for Sha Na Na. They were not theater people, all were experienced in their trades, get-the-job-done guys, and without them our shows would have been nowhere near as successful as they were. Fifty-five-plus communities are loaded with competent mechanics that have loads of experience and are eager to put their talents to work.

If you are working with kids or young people, you're going to have to hope that you've got someone like John Kaluta on board, who can help guide them through any technical projects. John's book, *The Perfect Stage Crew: The Compleat Technical Guide for High School, College, and Community Theater*, has lots of advice about how to construct and paint various set pieces. If you are into DYI, you should check it out. (See "Recommended Reading," appendix D, for more information.)

☆ What We Learned ☆

The first person to look to is the one who is most experienced in the venue you select. He will know the idiosyncrasies of the mechanical systems, the limits of the circuit breakers and electrical setup, and what is needed to overcome the limitations. He will also know what modifications can be made to the building without violating the policies of the landlords. If you are renting a theater, this person will probably be known as the technical director. (See appendix A for a helpful list of tips.)

☆ Stories from the Stage ☆

At 3 A.M. one morning, I was painting the Broadway drop for Guys and Dolls *on a descending well-type paint frame, where the drop was below the floor level. It was late, I was tired, and accidentally kicked over the bucket of black dye we were using for lining. It went on a diagonal in several lines across the drop. After staring at this catastrophic situation for several minutes, I had an inspiration and started painting black thin lines of driving rain across Broadway. On the closing night of the musical, the scenic designer came up to me and candidly said he couldn't remember why he had designed the drop for a rainy night. I never told him.*

—Norman Boulanger, lighting director and author of
Theatre Lighting from A to Z,
British Columbia

☆ Carpentry ☆

An experienced carpenter and a dedicated crew can oversee most construction needs. If your venue does not have a stage, your first thought might be to build your own. You should carefully consider whether you really need a platform stage. Visibility is a key issue. If your audience will be sitting on chairs that are all on the same level as the performers, the people in the back are not going to be able to see, so you may need a stage. If your audience is going to sit on tiered seating (such as risers in a gymnasium), you may not need to consider stage construction. Before making this decision about buying or renting a stage, research the options. Most rental companies have portable stages available in a multitude of sizes. Compare cost of building versus renting.

If your choice is to build a stage, many carpenters have lumber they may be willing to donate. They would decide on size and construct it in three or four sections so it can be transported if necessary. If you do choose to build your own stage, remember it will require a lot of under bracing to hold props, cast, crew, band, and piano. One option is to build a slightly smaller stage and have the musicians on the floor off to the side of the stage. Your carpenter will advise you to build in modules small enough to move and store, which is an excellent idea. This also applies to sets if you don't have a permanent venue where they can be stored.

☆ Sets and Props ☆

Speaking of sets, keep them simple and light. With a variety show, you need very little in terms of sets. Using a curtain as a background allows you to keep your construction to a minimum. If your space is already set up to be a theater, there is probably a system of pipes from which a curtain is already hanging, and there is probably a place where you could hang your own decorative background if you chose to do so. Depending upon your venue, and whether you are zero budget or big budget, you could also define and "dress" your space by having your crew build "flats" (basically, walls built out of muslin—don't try this without guidance) or even by setting up screens or using existing partitions, or even freestanding blackboards, and covering them with pictures or fabric.

If you are producing a scripted play or musical, you may need more elaborate sets. Each act might require individual props, and in some cases, set and lighting changes. Don't forget the wisdom learned by watching groups like the celebrated Paperbag Players. This troupe has been entertaining children and families for decades and their sets, made of paper bags, cardboard, and common household objects continue to delight. Necessity is the mother of invention, and creativity can trump construction. If you don't have access to expert carpenters, or an enormous budget, you can still have sets.

For the fourth-grade plays, we kept sets and props to a minimum. The fewer things children have to hold, move, and keep track of, the better. We used imagination and simple backdrops made of paper and cardboard. After a few years, we built permanent, freestanding flats that were light and easy to store. We repainted them each year with appropriate scenes. Changing background scenes is cumbersome and time consuming for little guys, so we used a "generic" scene that would support the theme of the play.

One of the things you may want to consider in creating sets is how you are going to get them on and off the stage. As you saw from John Kaluta's anecdote in the beginning of the chapter, big sets can cause big delays, and the movements have to be carefully choreographed. If you are very ambitious and have skilled and eager builders, maybe even an engineer, you might want to consider a turntable. Turning sets have become quite popular, for big shows—musicals like *Les Misérables*—as this cuts down on construction, movement, and other complications. Turning sets can be used in variety shows, but aren't really necessary, as the people onstage are the main focus. In a scripted play or musical, the sets become an integral part of the presentation, and choreographing a smooth set change may be one of the challenges you will need to face.

You may need to build props. In one scene, we needed a huge clock with large numbers, which was constructed by our crew. It was made of lightweight material and the construction crew figured out a way to hang it and remove it quickly at the right moment. Most props for variety shows will be handheld. Furniture should probably be used only when necessary, and then just enough of it to suggest a location—the occasional table, chair, or sofa.

Some acts will require a special backdrop. These can be easily constructed on wood frames with a canvas covering (the flats mentioned on page 71) that can be painted again and again. They are easily moved and stored, although storage can become a problem, as few people want to relinquish their garages and attics for this purpose. It is better to use your imagination whenever possible. If a person onstage says, "Look! There's an elephant!" the audience will look where the actor is pointing and see an elephant in their minds. This is especially true in children's productions as the fewer props they have to manipulate the less chance of dropping things and disrupting the flow of the story. For some reason, people think it is funny when props are dropped in front of a live audience. It may be comical, but if it isn't part of the act, it is simply disruptive.

✰ As Always, Expect the Unexpected ✰

It is important to have a carpenter with his tools during the show as unexpected needs arise. Just as the costume team needs to have scissors, pins, and tape, the construction crew should be available at a moment's notice with hammers, nails, and screwdrivers. For the show to run smoothly always be prepared for the unexpected and handle it quietly, casually, and quickly. These qualities will usually be found in your lead mechanics. At least one carpenter needs to be at rehearsals and all performances.

✰ Stories from the Stage ✰

The lighting designer was at his wits' end with a last minute change in blocking that had the actor come down the theater aisle reciting his lines. The designer had neither a lighting instrument nor a dimmer available anywhere in the theater. So he did what designers have always talked about in private. He put a colored gel over the lighted end of a flashlight. He then instructed the actor to walk down the aisle holding the flashlight on his face. It worked! Sometimes the simplest solution is the best.

—Norman Boulanger, *lighting director and author of*
Theatre Lighting from A to Z,
British Columbia

☆ Lighting and Electrical ☆

Lighting is one of the most important aspects of the whole production. Lighting, along with music, creates the mood for the audience, and directs the focus on what is happening on that stage. People become disgruntled when they can't see the action or if the stage is so dimly lit, they have to squint and ask, "What's he doing?" This is an area that requires a lighting expert, as it is the lighting that directs the audience's vision.

When doing a scripted play or musical, the lighting becomes more complicated and must be planned to the last detail. There is so much to be done creatively with lighting. It makes your scripted play or variety show come alive. With proper lighting, the stage can go from day to night. A spotlight on a dark stage adds intrigue and mystery. Colored lights create a whole different ambiance for a scene.

Lighting is not an area in which to skimp. If your venue doesn't have proper lighting, this is where you need to spend some money on rentals, or get some imaginative people who can improvise. We have tried using lightbulbs in coffee cans when money was tight, but realized during dress rehearsal that coffee cans just won't cut it. We had to bite the bullet and spend some money to rent and borrow proper lighting.

Aside from making the audience uncomfortable when they can't see clearly, the cast members onstage become frustrated, as they know their act is being compromised by poor lighting. After putting in hours and hours of work and rehearsals, they want to be seen in all their glory. Applause is louder when everything is properly illuminated. Aside from the actual performance, the lighting directly affects the quality of the video. If the video has ample light, the acts appear as they were onstage rather than appearing to be under water or in a snowfall.

If you are using theatrical lights, you are going to need a lighting designer, an electrician, people to hang the lights, and people to run the lighting board during the show. You need the lighting designer because if you go through the expense of renting theatrical lights, you probably want the person who decides where they should go to be an expert in making the most out of them. You want the lighting plot to provide the best, most even illumination; you want the light to make your performers not only visible, but also attractive; you want lighting effects to be as well conceived as possible.

You need an electrician, because you're going to be using a lot of electricity, and you want to make sure your facility can handle it (the technical director of the space may be the person who can help you here). Any rented lights need to be hung from pipes in the ceiling (or maybe set up on the floor or on pipes on the side of the stage). They need to be cabled and plugged in, and they need to be focused. That's why you need a crew. And you'll need to allot time to get those lights hung in the space. The on and off of all those lights are controlled by a lighting board. That's why you need a board operator, someone who can make the lights go on and off at the right time. If you are using follow spots—spotlights that will follow your singers and dancers around the stage—you're going to need follow-spot operators.

The people operating the lights must have clear directions written down on a technical script so they can get the timing exactly right. They must have the script strategically marked with every single lighting requirement highlighted for the entire show. This includes the opening, every act, intermission, and closing. Fade-in, fade-out lights are effective when used at the proper moment. You never want an actor standing onstage mutely waiting for the lights to be adjusted. The lighting team should get specific directions and a lot of praise for a job well done.

If all of this sounds highly technical—it is. But don't despair, there are a lot of books out there that can give you information about lighting, and there are lots of people in your community who have some lighting knowledge. John Kaluta's book has terrific basic lighting information, as does *Technical Theater for Nontechnical People*, by Drew Campbell. (See "Recommended Reading," appendix D.)

These days, lighting can be unbelievably sophisticated. Most boards are run by a computer, and the most elaborate effects can be generated. But remember the flashlight story from the beginning of this section. Sometimes the simplest solution is the right one. There used to be a popular, underground show in New York City called *And That's How the Rent Gets Paid*. Sometimes the proprietors didn't (pay the rent, that is) and they would ask the audience to bring along flashlights, which served as the only source of illumination. The enthusiasm of the fans was not diminished, even if the theater lights were.

☆ Stories from the Stage ☆

As an audio technician for a large metropolitan church, I was part of a team responsible for providing sound for all services and specials. This included both the operation of equipment and routine maintenance required on old equipment, to stretch its life span out a little longer. We also produced a TV show of the Sunday services every week so several people were involved behind the scenes on any given Sunday. We were always a little anxious before a big event. Even though the equipment had been checked and re-checked many times, much of it was old and you never knew when it would give up.

Over the years, we had experienced equipment failure during big events and they were never fun. On a particular Easter Sunday, we were all attuned to every nuance of the program. We proceeded flawlessly through two services and were just starting to relax a bit, knowing we were on the home stretch, when, without warning, the power went out.

It was a bright day outside and our Sanctuary windows provide plenty of light. Most people did not immediately notice. The sound system, however, demanded electricity, and we had none. The crew leaped into action, checking electrical panels for blown breakers. No luck. We called the power company to see if they had a problem. The news wasn't good. A transformer had blown and there would be no power for the entire region until late afternoon.

We couldn't just tear down and go home as we had another service to do. Even without amplifying the sound, providing stage lighting, or video-taping the service, it still had to go on. We shut down power to all gear to protect from surges when the power did come back. We were all relieved that the beginning of the service could be done acoustically.

We had a choir, a grand piano, and acoustic drums. It could work—at least for the beginning of the service. The big performance song before the message would be a problem, though. With a soloist being backed by the choir and a full band, the soloist would be lost in the choir voices.

But there was nothing we could do. Without electricity we had no way to amplify anything. The primary sound operator, having nothing to do at his mixing board, was in the recording booth with the camera operators, relaxing and having a snack. We couldn't go home because it was part of our job to clean up the stage after the service ended. With nothing more we could do, we all drifted back to our respective places.

It was, for each of them, at least a place to sit down in a standing-room crowd. It seems we'd no sooner resumed our positions, and with no more warning than when we'd lost power, suddenly it was back on! There was a swell of thunderous applause and cheering from down the hall in the sanctuary. With a pause just long enough to make sure it wasn't going to go right back out, we frantically started turning things back on. From the record decks to the video production bay to the stage lights, we flipped switches, loaded tapes, and readied ourselves to pick up the pieces of a short-circuited performance. We were back in business.

—Liah Rose, sound technician, Portland, Oregon

☆ Sound ☆

The advice on sound that we received from Liah is so excellent, thorough, and detailed, we have decided to include it exactly as she sent it to us:

The first thing I assess in a possible venue is where the power outlets are, especially in relation to the stage. This is especially important in outdoor events, where adequate power must be delivered to a remote site, and could even affect the positioning of the stage. The location of outlets contributes to deciding both where I will position myself to run the sound, but also where to position the speakers (since the particular speakers I use require an electrical hookup). Smaller venues with limited outlets can usually be accommodated with heavy-duty extension cords, as long as those outlets don't have a limited capacity. Most venues these days, though, have plenty of outlets, with a pretty high capacity as well.

Once I have established the venue, big or small, the next big piece of information is what the show will entail. How many people will be performing? What is the nature of the performance? How will each portion of the show begin and end? Will there be musical instruments? What are the specific needs of each instrument to hook into a sound system? This information helps me to establish what equipment will be required. Specifically how many microphones and what type of microphones (wireless or wired, handheld or lavalier) will be needed.

With this information in hand, I am then able to assess whether or not I will need to acquire additional mikes, cables, stands, or other gear. Then I find out how early on the day of the event I will be able to have access to the room in order to set up the sound. As the event nears, I double check that everything is in working order, and also verify that I have all the extras I need (like batteries or extra connectors). For a large event, I plan to arrive at the venue three to four hours before the room is scheduled to be opened for the event. For smaller events, in a familiar venue, that time might be cut to as little as ninety minutes, but is typically around two to three hours. A complex operation can take this long to set up and test. Even a simple set up requires the cables be taped down or "dressed" so they are out of the way and not a hazard to the performers.

Sound and electrical come together at the connections, just as electrical merges with lighting. But once the connections are made, and the power is delivered, you need someone who understands mikes, boards, speakers, and controls.

☆ Helpful Hint ☆

When you have chosen your venue, co-directors are advised to take the lighting and sound experts with them to inspect the theater. They can then make a list of things needed to adequately light and provide sound for the show.

Although it sounds easy to say, "Oh, we'll just put up some lights and get a few microphones," it becomes obvious this won't be good enough. Light bulbs in coffee cans may be cheap, but your show will reflect this when the audience can't see or hear what is happening onstage. Sound and lights are extremely complicated and can't be left to chance; that's why you need to find experts.

☆ Your Tech Team ☆

As you can tell, construction is important, as is the setup of lighting and sound equipment. The team members who work during the actual show—your running crew—are crucial. In addition to any personnel needed to run the lighting board, focus the follow spots, control the sound, and move the sets, at least one team member who can troubleshoot will be needed during dress rehearsal and the performances.

The most important thing is these people must work together as a cohesive team because more often than not, a problem in one area will cause problems in others.

CHAPTER 10

Writing Your Script

Even if your show is strictly in the variety show format, and all your acts are self-contained, you are going to need some kind of "glue" to hold it together. You will need an announcer, or announcers, who can talk to the audience between acts and tell them what's upcoming. You will want your announcers to be entertaining, just as the rest of the show is. You might want them to crack a joke, or who knows, maybe even have some kind of a running theme going on. Don't worry, your writing team is going to supply the material that holds it all together.

☆ Stories from the Stage ☆

We took a group of junior high kids to a Tucson school for the last performance of a short cowboy spoof. The stand-in for the lead begged to play the part since he hadn't had a chance to be onstage. We told the lead, and of course, he agreed to stay home that day. We arrived at the school and set up our props and sound in the lunchroom. Everything was informal and out in the open. The audience was seated; our kids were in chairs alongside the "stage." As the actors moved out to take their places, someone in the first row yelled, "Hey, dude, you look weird in that cowboy outfit!" The stand-in froze. He didn't speak. He didn't move. He just stood. The prompter gave him his lines and he still refused to speak. Since the lead wasn't there, we were at a loss as to what to do. Very quietly, one of the extras, a square dancer, stepped up and said, "I know all the lines. I've been listening during rehearsals." The stand-in was happy to stand down and the "extra" gave a perfect performance!

—Evelyn Franke, theater director, Tucson, Arizona

☆ What We Did ☆

When we started this project we knew a talent show with an emcee announcing a series of acts was not what we wanted. Our goals were to involve as many people as possible, provide local color, and present an excellent show. We had a great stroke of good luck. *The Tonight Show* with Johnny Carson was the most popular late night show on television and this show met all our goals and provided the flexible structure. We used the Carson format throughout all our shows, and we were lucky to have Ken Sargent who played Johnny in every one.

We started the show with this structure in mind because it was so flexible, provided a format for writing monologues, introductions, and skits, and allowed us to begin searching for acts at the very beginning of the process. Using this variety format we could include acts from chimpanzees to the Beatles. (In one show we actually had a woman in a gorilla costume onstage!) We wanted to have cute little kids from the local dance class and professionals like Chris Clark, a bass guitar player who spent his professional career as a studio musician backing up singers in Nashville and Los Angeles.

All acts were welcome to audition, and everyone could fit into this format. The beauty of a variety show was that it allowed the acts to showcase their individual talents while we were writing the introductions, transitions, and commercials that would bind the show together and create material that would reach the community.

However, you may want to choose a scripted drama or musical to begin with. We have both produced and participated in numerous scripted plays and performed in variety shows produced for fundraising. Each form has merits.

☆ What We Learned ☆

We truly did not know how lucky we were. The choice of an open-ended variety show was ideal for writing a script that would allow us to lampoon and involve all the characteristics of the community and the people who lived there. We were always careful to get a laugh at their foibles, but to be sure they were laughing *with* us. They loved it. The second stroke of good luck was that we rounded up a group of people with some real comic "sense," and the sensitivity to know the limits.

Many people are totally unaware that writing comedy is one of the most difficult and delicate writing tasks. You must be funny *and* careful. You must also think about the audience that you are addressing. If you are writing a show for the entire family, you are probably using different standards, concerning what's allowable and what's funny, than you would be if you were writing for a senior community. If you are writing for an all-college-age crowd, as do the students in the comedy club Poptards at Marymount Manhattan College in New York, your standards and your references are not going to be the same as they would be if you were writing for their parents. As we look back we see the many benefits of writing our own scripts and using the variety show format. (See appendix A for a helpful list of tips.)

✰ Benefits of Writing Your Own Variety Show ✰

- You have a larger cast, which gives you more word-of-mouth publicity in the community
- The script can be localized for your group
- You can insert local commercials and gags that will create great response
- Participants are not required to rehearse as a group over a long period of time
- Individual acts and novices are only required to prepare for their five or seven minutes onstage
- It is a grassroots creation
- Each act is responsible for props, music, and costumes with little assistance required

We decided on a variety show because the community was small, but loaded with lots of talented people, and, living on an island, many unique, quirky situations—long ferry lines, throngs of tourists in summer months, and living with all our friends and neighbors through the long, dark winter. They were apparent to all and provided plenty of fodder for a writing group. We used the fact we lived on a popular, destination resort island. When 200 cyclists left the ferry and traveled seventeen miles to the main town, the roads were clogged for hours. Tourists brought lots of money with them, which we gladly accepted, but were still the main object of scorn. There were two taverns, a few restaurants licensed to serve alcohol, and one stoplight on the island.

We contacted a group of people we thought could contribute to writing the script. We did not look for "writers." *We knew the final script would be in our hands, and we knew this would be important.* We looked for people with either a history in the community, newcomers to the island experience, or a connection with current activities, and, most of all, a sense of humor about it all.

Eight to ten of us gathered together at Gail's house. We explained the goals, the show, and what we were trying to do with the script. Everyone had ideas for skits, based on everything from living on an island to global warming. We brainstormed ideas that concerned local "characters," local politics, and the most recent crazy events. We all offered material, made humorous comments, and suggested skits, many of which we were forced to leave on the cutting room floor.

At the end of the evening, most of the material was still in concept with some specific dialogue, gags, and skits in first draft form. The group members took the ideas with them and came back the next week. In the meantime, we wrote and developed the ideas, took them back to the group, had another amazingly productive, humorous session, and "finalized" the script. That was the *first* final script, which was then gone over by Gail, Colleen, and Gail's husband, Doug, to produce the final. We met for a final review and ended up with a working script.

The script focuses on three things: introductions and transitions between acts, commercials, and banter between the emcee and his side-kick. We recommend the emcee have a sidekick because dialogue is an easy way to provide information, and the give and take is a great way to set up jokes and gags. During one show, a running gag was about a remodeling job to one of the most popular restaurants in town. More on that later.

Introduction and Transitions

We used a Ed McMahon and Johnny Carson style of banter and always started with the standard Ed introduction of Johnny. "Johnny" would welcome the audience, swing his golf club, maybe tell a joke about the current state of the island, and move right into the first act. Johnny always made the transitions between acts and we kept those down to minimal dialogue, because we felt it was important to keep the show moving at a good pace. In fact, we believe that the pace of the show contributed greatly to its success. We always tried to combine the acts, intermission, and the material we wrote into a two-hour package.

Banter

The banter between Johnny and Ed was always kept to a minimum since the goal was to move on to the next act. We copied the Karnak segment many times because it was short and adaptable. For example, Carmac was a local company named after the two owners, Carlson and MacIntyre, so Johnny would be decked in a turban as "Carmac, the Magnificent." He would then do the routine with the answer in the envelope and the question provided by Ed on an index card. Johnny would read, "The answer is 'Earth, Wind, and Fire.' " Johnny would then hold the envelope with the question to his turban, ponder the answer as if he was receiving messages from the beyond, frown, and proclaim, "The question is, What does one get after dining at Bilbo's Mexican Restaurant?" Drum roll. Another answer: "Moran State Park." Once again, Johnny would perform the ritual and say, "The question is, Where do newcomers searching for affordable housing go after they leave the real estate offices in Eastsound?"

Commercials

Since we were doing a television format, we knew the show needed commercials, and the local businesses provided great content and excellent targets for some gentle satire. Of course, we didn't charge money for these as they were scripted as part of the show. The audience loved them and by the time we were planning our second show, local businesses were asking if they could be included. Of course, you may want to charge for commercials as a way of increasing revenue for your fundraiser.

CHAPTER 11

Choosing a Scripted Show

If you decide you want to try your hand at directing a scripted show, some challenges you face will be the same; some will be entirely different. You and your cast will be re-interpreting a script that has already been performed by others. Your cast will need to learn lines and movement. They will need to take on characters and present the story to the audience so that it moves them, or makes them laugh, or whatever the playwright intended.

⋆ Stories from the Stage ⋆

Here's another story from our experiences. My husband, Doug, and I were directing the junior class play one year so the kids could raise money for their Spring Prom. They chose The Curious Savage. *All went well for the Friday and Saturday night performances, but the cast and crew saw the Sunday matinee as a "throwaway." The audience was sparse and the teenagers got the giggles and flubbed some lines. That snowballed and the curtain puller began pulling the curtain back and forth just to befuddle the actors. When two cast members stepped onstage wearing funny hats, we had seen enough. We walked to center stage and told the audience their money would be refunded at the door, as they weren't getting the quality show they had paid to see.*

The play continued and the actors shaped up in a hurry and although a few audience members accepted their refund, most of them refused and said, "A good lesson was learned here today. It was worth the five bucks!"

—Gail Brown, teacher, author, and director,
Casa Grande, Arizona

☆ The Pros and Cons of Working with a Script ☆

First advantage, obviously, you do not have to write a script. A playwright will have already thought his way through the script and, in most cases, the play will already have been staged numerous times, which means a director and actors will have already worked their way through the physical actions of the play, and these actions will have been dutifully noted by the stage manager. The published script will contain all of this information, which might make the play easier to stage.

The cast of a variety show could contain fifty people or more; the cast of a scripted show is usually much smaller. A smaller cast means fewer people to organize, direct, and rehearse, which seems like an advantage at first. However, a smaller cast also means a smaller "captive" audience—fewer family and friends. By default, it also means that you are probably going to be "non-inclusive"; not everybody who wants to perform on the stage is going to get a part. You might try to find a script that had parts for everyone who wished to participate, but that in itself could be a major undertaking.

If you are producing a play, particularly a musical, you probably have a known commodity that has worked for other theater groups. A popular musical ensures audience identification with the production. The publisher who licenses the musical will provide scores, charts, and promotional material is available. Do remember royalties must be paid and you need to figure them into your bottom line.

Also, be aware that the format of a scripted play often means that audience interest must be maintained for longer stretches of time. The action of a play or a musical unfolds over the course of an hour or more, and your audience will have to be able to remain engaged and to understand what is happening. That means your actors will need to sustain their concentration, and their performances. If you are working with inexperienced actors, you need to have the confidence, and the skills, as a director, to lead them through it.

One other thought: although the cast might be smaller, the rehearsal process will probably be more of a logistical nightmare. If you're planning on performing *Oliver* you may need to organize group rehearsals, nearly every night, for a period of two months! Think of the scheduling conflicts! If your acts can be rehearsed individually, you obviously won't have to do this. Variety shows also cut down on rental time for rehearsals.

☆ Choosing a Scripted Show ☆

There are all kinds of amateur and semi-professional groups out there presenting plays. Many are established institutions with a lengthy history; some groups have smaller ambitions. Most community theater groups that need to raise funds to continue operating or to raise money for another worthy cause will choose to present a scripted play or musical. Groups that have been together a long time have the knowledge and wherewithal to choose the most appropriate plays or musicals to present during their upcoming season. The choice depends on a number of things.

The budget for the production will determine the selection, as newer scripts are costly and usually out of range for smaller theater groups. Plays or musicals such as *Annie* or *Oklahoma* will cost less than newer shows such as *The Lion King* or *Cats*.

Choosing shows for an entire season must be done a year or longer in advance, because it takes time to put everything in place. Rights to the plays and musicals must be obtained, royalties paid, and there will be many phone calls back and forth before the season is set. The biggest challenge is to find scripts that are not only affordable, but will draw the audience and ensure that the seats are filled for all performances. Some theater groups call the older, reliable scripts "workhorses" as they have been presented many times by many groups and are affordable. The plus side here is potential attendees are familiar with the plays and have a sense of security in knowing what to expect.

According to our experienced friends in theater groups, most people who will purchase tickets prefer musicals to serious dramatic productions. If there is an unknown title on the season's roster, it alone might prevent potential season ticket buyers from buying the whole package.

Theater groups generally expand and include new material or more challenging shows as they experiment and broaden their base. The directors and actors want to stretch their wings and move away from the "workhorses," but in doing so, they risk losing viewers because people often say, "I go to the theater to be entertained and I don't want to sit through some avant garde show I know nothing about." Sticking with the tried and true has its advantages. The final decisions have to be based on budget, ability to obtain rights to the works, the group's mission, and the audience appeal. This is a huge undertaking and one that can be handled by those with a good deal of experience in theater.

If the community theater is small, one production for the year might be all it can afford. In this case, the selection of "the one" becomes paramount to the success of the fundraiser. Questions have to

be asked to guide those in charge of selection. Who is your target audience? If you are performing in a small town where more conservative
theatergoers will be purchasing tickets, this must be considered. Do you
have a big city population from which to draw? What has worked well
in the past? *Joseph and the Amazing Technicolor Dreamcoat* draws
crowds, but the prospective ticket buyers might have seen one too
many musicals and be ready for a serious, dramatic play. This is a tight
rope to walk and the person who makes the final selection probably will
consult with the board of directors, actors, directors, and former season
ticket holders. Ultimately, the decision has to be made on past history,
budget, availability, and the potential audience.

If your group does decide to present a scripted play or musical, the
co-directors must have a team meeting and give input on making the
final selection.

CHAPTER 12

Ideas for Acts in a Variety Show

Each act makes its own unique statement and diversity is the key. We are including a list of acts that take the audience to many different places. The secret is to choose something for everyone in the audience.

☆ Stories from the Stage ☆

I had everything planned for a perfect talent show. Children of every age had auditioned and the show was a great mix of all kinds of talent: singers, dancers, ventriloquists, jugglers, everything I could find. Performance time was perfect for a young audience. At the last minute, a woman I knew well approached me and said her family had been out of town during auditions and her daughter was in tears and inconsolable because she wouldn't get to be in the show. I had seen her daughter perform previously and knew she was an excellent tap dancer, so I reluctantly added her name to the roster at the last minute.

Her act was third on the program and I felt confident she would do well. Her performance was fine, but since I had not seen the act, I was shocked when her number went on and on. After ten minutes, I had to do the "finger across the throat" indicating it was time to cut it off! Apparently, the pianist didn't understand theater sign language and the act continued for an additional three full minutes. Since that day, I have always insisted on auditioning each act before the curtains open!

—Michael Woodruff, director and producer, Children's Plays,
Monroe, Louisiana

☆ What We Did ☆

We based our show on Johnny Carson because it was the big-hit variety show on TV at the time. Today, if you were using our talk show format, you might choose Ellen DeGeneres or Jay Leno. You could also choose an *American Idol*–type talent show (more on this in chapter 20). You could also use a "reality show" format, provided it was viewer appropriate, or even a more confrontational talk show, like *Oprah* or *Dr. Phil*, once again, considering whether that would be offensive to your audience. If your show is heavily comedic, a *Saturday Night Live* setup might work. Our show was called "Orcas Tonight." The more you personalize to your community or organization, the easier it is to create ideas and personalize the theme.

☆ What We Learned ☆

As the shows went by, we added material to our inventory. Some pieces we kept, some we discarded, and every year, we came up with new acts. Many were created by people who participated in previous shows, and a few new groups would show up every year with ideas.

☆ Examples of Popular Acts ☆

Over the years, we have used the some of the following acts in our productions.

Scripted Skits

We wrote to the *Carol Burnett Show* requesting material for our fundraiser and received a complete script we could use without paying royalties. We only used a ten-minute segment called "Sorry" and it was presented as written and was a real crowd pleaser due to the familiarity with the characters. The folks at the *Burnett Show* understood what we were doing, were enthusiastic about the project, and wanted to contribute to the show.

Some of your performers might want to write their own skits. The Poptards (the college comedy group we mentioned earlier) wrote a skit about all the characters you meet on the subway in New York. Since most of the audience members were freshmen, brand new to New York and experiencing subway weirdos for the first time, the skit had a lot of resonance.

Female Singing and Dancing Routine

Pick a group that is currently popular and change the name to something pertinent to your organization or community. Select a medley of old and/or new material that relates to a diversified audience. One of our female singing and dancing routines involved a group that was popular at the time, the Pointer Sisters. We changed the name to the Setter Sisters and they sang a medley of songs recorded by the Pointer Sisters.

Novelty Act: Dem Bones

Here's an idea you can give to a group that is eager to perform, but does not have an act of its own. Start with three people in black leotards with white felt bones Velcroed to their bodies. The two people on the sides have bones attached to their backs. The center person has the bones attached to her front. The trio stands side by side with their backs to the audience. As the "Dem Bones" song begins, the two side people take the appropriate bone off the front of the middle person and put it on the person's back, thus building the skeleton in unison with the song. When this is complete, all three will have bones on their backs and their backs will be facing the audience. At the conclusion of the song, a black light comes on and the audience gasps as all they can see are bones dancing onstage. Repeat the "Dem Bones" song. This is a unique and exciting act.

Singing Guy Group

Choose a popular group from any genre of pop music. It is exciting to have a large group of five or six men. We chose Sha Na Na and added a female dancer to be Runaround Sue. We began with the men onstage. Then Sue made her appearance at the appropriate moment in the song. Today, you could choose hip-hop or rap stars, boy bands, or a group like the Black Eyed Peas, which would include both male and female singers and dancers.

Helpful Hint: This is a great group to use as the last act before intermission. It gets the audience exhilarated and excited to see what is coming next. This kind of act involves the crowd, as they tend to clap and sing along. As they recognize friends, relatives, and acquaintances onstage, they begin to become involved as active participants. It leaves the audience full of enthusiasm as they gather in the foyer during intermission. Our Sha Na Na performers were so well received that in the next show we produced their repertoire was increased to three numbers.

Jazz Trio

We had senior citizens performing jazz songs from yesteryear. Of course, your instrumentalists don't have to be seniors, and the music doesn't have to be jazz—although those old standards are real crowd pleasers. This could also include a singer.

Ballroom Dance Routine

Have a couple dancing rumba, tango, swing, or the dance of your choice. Our dancers chose their music and choreographed their own dance, as they had participated in several dance contests. They designed and made their own costumes.

Country Singer Group or Duo

You can use country songs that are current or from days gone by. Suggestions for singers include Alan Jackson, Kenny Chesney, Faith Hill, Tim McGraw, Gretchen Wilson, Oak Ridge Boys, Alabama, Dolly Parton, Johnny Cash, etc. What about local performers? Perhaps someone in your town is a locally famous entertainer who can perform his/her own rendition of a musical selection. It could be an original or cover song.

When a person we know wrote a parody poking fun at San Juan Airlines, he used "North to Alaska" and changed it to "North on San Juan Air." The whole song was re-written to be community specific.

Female Diva Vocalist

We opened our show with a Barbra Streisand imitator who sang an original song designed to introduce "Orcas Tonight." She was the first act. The song expressed a welcome to the audience and gratitude for attending our fundraising variety show. It was inviting, welcoming and kicked the show off heralding things to come.

More Dance Routines

A soft shoe routine, with or without vocals, can be engaging. Tap is a crowd pleaser, and can be performed by adults, teens, or tiny tots. If you have a local dance studio, it might be able to provide the talent—and the routines.

Something for the Kids

Consult with your kids about what is "in" at the moment. Create a skit where the performers dress like Muppets, Dora the Explorer, the Teletubbies, Spongebob Squarepants, Kim Possible—little kids will delight in recognizing their favorite characters, just as the adults delight in movie and TV star impersonations.

Stand-up Comedy Routine

If you choose to have a stand-up comedy routine, you must realize comedy is the most difficult to write and pull off onstage. Someone could impersonate Ray Romano, Chris Rock, Joan Rivers, or Margaret Cho. They can catch these comics on TV and write some material that is similar to the celebrity's or they can write their own material and just be themselves. You're better off if you use stand-up comedians with some experience (or, at least some experience with making speeches—Toastmasters members, people like that). If you have performers who want to try out their comedic skills, you should suggest that they rehearse their material—and test it out in front of a smaller audience, before the dress rehearsal.

Barbershop Quartet

Most places have four men with good voices who are either already performing in a Barbershop Quartet, or you can put one together for the show. They can borrow costumes from people who are in a quartet, or find their own red and white–striped blazers, white pants, and straw hats.

Magic Act

This is a good place for a youngster who is interested in magic to perform. A couple of books on magic tricks can be found in the library and three or four tricks with scarves, coins, water glasses, and a fake rabbit in the hat will be enough.

Juggler

There is generally someone around who knows how to juggle four or five oranges. This should be very short with lively musical accompaniment. This act can be used to fill in a bit of time as a more intricate act is getting ready to perform.

Other Music Styles

The possibilities are limited only by the talents of your performers and the tastes of your audiences. Blue grass, hip-hop, rap, rock 'n' roll, heavy metal, pop, Latin, chamber music . . . not everything has to be popular music, and not everything has to be a group. A solo performer could play piano, fiddle, accordion clarinet, sax, bagpipes, drum solo, saw . . . whatever expertise allows. A gospel choir or other choral group involving a large number of people could be very exciting.

Roller Skaters

A pair of skaters dressed in tights with the female in a tutu. We used a teenager on roller skates to hold up a sign throughout the show designating applause, intermission, commercial breaks, and the end of the show.

Fake Commercials

These are like skits, but they can be extremely short. Everyone loves to hate commercials, and everyone loves to see commercials skewered. You can use these short, funny bits as filler and transitions between larger acts. In fact, if you stage it carefully, you can actually have a two-person commercial performed down in the front of the stage (that's "downstage") while stagehands are *quietly* setting up an act behind them ("upstage"). In the theater, a scene like this is called "in two" and that is exactly what those two-person, limited-location scenes are for—covering transitions.

Real Commercials

This is a way to add spice and originality to your show. It can also bring in added revenue if you choose to charge. Commercials can be used as a way to honor businesses or corporations that have sponsored your fundraiser with their generous donations. A total of five short commercials seems to fit well with the flow of the show. This is a perfect area to get creative and spotlight local businesses. Our commercials were made into short skits.

One skit we did showed the local grocery store where various groups set up tables to raise funds. Veterans sold poppies on Veterans' Day, raffle tickets were sold to benefit the library, Girl Scouts sold cookies, and the Lions sold tickets to upcoming events. The Lions Club member was dressed in a fabulous lion headpiece, the Girl Scouts wore their outfits, and the Veterans wore their uniforms. A harried shopper rushed in to buy her groceries, but stopped at every booth to purchase something before entering the store. By the time she got to the check-out with her grocery cart full, she discovered she was completely out of cash. The tag line was, "Shop at Templin's Grocery Store where we serve the entire community!"

Another favorite was the running-gag commercial. When we did these, no other commercials were used in that particular show. We interspersed the quick skits throughout the performance. For example, there was an extraordinarily good Mexican Restaurant named Bilbo's that attracted those who love South of the Border cuisine. One year, they remodeled the restaurant and construction was supposed to be completed in a couple of months. In our commercial, a Bilbo's fanatic arrived on the scene dressed in summer clothing and asked when she could expect to enjoy the Number One dinner on the menu. The man who was doing the remodeling was a perfectionist and replied, "Soon. Very soon. Look, do you think I should use *this* nail or *this* nail? Which would be better?" "Either one," she replied, "Just get it done!" A few acts later, she appeared in fall clothing and received the same response. Her next appearance was in Christmas regalia and the builder said, "Have patience. This is an act of love." Finally, she came back on in summer clothes once again and said, "*When* is Bilbo's going to reopen!?" The builder looked at her and said, "Oh, they opened last month while you were away on vacation. Now they're closed again so the owners can take a break!" Everyone could relate to this exaggerated skit because they were all eager to have some of that delicious food. The owners thought the spoof was funny and the audience loved it. (We did check with the owners before we incorporated the skit.)

Another commercial was for Ray's Pharmacy. Three young women dressed as Vitamins A, B, and C. The pharmacy owner's young son acted as the emcee and introduced each vitamin, which recited a short poem about its usefulness and ended with a little dance and the line, "We're the ABCs of Ray's Pharmacy!"

Our "live" commercials were always a big hit.

Mime

This space will be left "silent" in honor of the mime.

Tummies

This is a spectacular act to close your production. It became our sig-nature ending with the costumes becoming more elaborate each year and more guys clamoring to participate. Because of the popular appeal of this act, we're going to give you explicit directions for staging it. We hope it proves to be the applause-getter for you that it was for us.

Choose men with prominent bellies and one man with a slender physique. The men hold their arms straight above their heads so the makeup artist can apply the "face." Large, red puckered lips are painted around the belly button to represent whistling mouths. Add eyes and noses to complete the face. Foam or paper ears are taped to their torsos at the waist with adhesive tape. Flesh-colored makeup foundation covers the tape.

Hats are constructed by using large plastic garbage cans covered with colored poster paper, flowers, stars and other decorations. Suit coats, shirts, and ties are draped around the hips, Suit-sleeves are stuffed with tissue paper, and gloves attached to the ends of the suit sleeves. The guy's arms, which are holding up the garbage can, are completely hidden by it. Their heads are also hidden. Elastic-banded pants are worn under the jackets exposing the bellies so the painted faces can be seen.

The men undulate their bellies to simulate whistling so it looks like the sound is coming from their belly buttons. We used the whistling version of "The Bridge Over the River Kwai" as accompaniment to this hysterical routine. The slapstick, raucous act left even the most sophisticated audience members laughing until tears rolled down their cheeks and wondering whose faces were under those hats.

Power Point or Slide Presentation

A montage is a great way to end a show if you decide not to use the Tummy Act. It can be done as a slide show or a PowerPoint presentation and is especially moving for a community or organization with a long history together. The team leader assembles pictures from days gone by up to current photographs. These are organized in chronological order. When we did this segment, the music we chose to accompany it was John Denver's "Friends." The words are "Friends, we will remember you, think of you, pray for you and when another day is through, we'll still be friends with you." A group of five people stood beside the stage and sang the song throughout the presentation, in very subdued lighting. Our local doctor softly played the harmonica in the background. We began with an island sunrise and closed with an island sunset. There were perfect bookends for the touching moments in the photographs.

☆ A Source of Inspiration ☆

We're offering you this list of things we did. Your team of writers can use what fits, improvise on one of our ideas, or ignore them all. The key is to use what works for you. These are just springboards to get your juices flowing. You might want to keep it up to date and use hip-hop, rap, and current music groups. It's fun to change the names of popular groups such as the Black Eyed Peas and call them the String Beans or call the Rolling Stones the Kidney Stones. Ideas for skits can be gleaned from *Mad Magazine* as they are always up to the minute with their parodies on popular TV shows and movies. Also, keeping a notepad beside the sofa as you watch TV will remind you of popular acts you might want to include in the show. You can also get some good jokes from the late-night talk show hosts. Be careful not to plagiarize anything or anybody. Get the idea, then spin it your way. If you personalize the jokes to fit members of your group, you'll come off sounding like a professional joke writer even if you aren't!

CHAPTER 13

....

Costumes, Hair, and Makeup

You are keeping your set to a minimum, and you've carefully counted each penny spent on equipment rentals. Here's an area where you can get colorful and creative without breaking the bank–personal adornment!! Otherwise known as costumes, hair, and makeup.

☆ Stories from the Stage ☆

The Cornerstone Theater Company was performing the Oresteia *in a town in Nevada on one of our regular summer tours. The performance was set up in a large metal building that housed an auto repair shop. It provided lots of space, and on one end, had auto-lift doors that allowed exits and entrances for scene and costume changes. What could go wrong?*

Amy Brenneman, star of Judging Amy, *was playing Clytemnestra, and in her climactic scene, had to exit, execute a lightning-fast costume change, and return with blood flowing from self-inflicted wounds. The assistant was busy securing the back of her costume, and Amy was dipping into a pot of "stage blood," staining her face and the front of her Greek tunic preparing for her entrance and her next line.*

Unfortunately, the can from which she was dipping, was a gallon bucket of motor oil. Smeared with motor oil and faced with an immediate entrance, Amy and the assistant quickly switched buckets, applied the red paint to the costume, and covered as much of the motor oil as possible. She hit her entrance in a tunic smeared with stage blood red applied over motor oil black. Perhaps one of the great anachronisms in Greek tragedy.

—Christopher Liam Moore, actor, director, and founding member,
Cornerstone Theater Company,
Los Angeles

✫ Another Story from the Stage ✫

Our community theater group was producing Cinderella, Belle of Boyle. *I was dressed in my lovely period costume. It consisted of a fuchsia and black bodice, long black gloves and a huge, black and fuchsia full-length hoop skirt. When it was time to make my exit, I twirled around and the hoop skirt got caught up in the curtains. I suddenly took a swan dive off the stage, bruised my chin and knocked a filling out of my tooth! During the Grande Finale I took my bows with my tongue holding the filling in place and tried to smile through the agony. I learned to be more careful in hoop skirts and not stand so close to the edge of the stage!*

—Anne Byrom, box office manager, West T. Hill Community Theatre,
Danville, Kentucky

✫ What We Did ✫

Most of our costumes were created by the participating groups, and consisted of whatever they had in their closets or could borrow from a neighbor. Some, however, would buy material, get out the sewing machines and create some great outfits. Only when some special item, like a wig or a period costume was needed, did we get involved. When asked, we would scout around, put out the word and, somehow or other, it would turn up rescued from a closet or an attic. If we could not find a particular item, someone who was going to town would stop at a costume shop and buy it.

The local beauty shop operator showed up every year and patiently did everyone in the show needing makeup or a hairdo. She eventually recruited a crew and they worked tirelessly to make sure the finishing touches were perfect before anyone went onstage. She still does hair and makeup for the Center.

✫ What We Learned ✫

We found that the team leaders for costumes, makeup, and hair all work together to get the job done. They share materials, ideas, and techniques. Their true value is displayed in the hour before the curtain rises for the first time.

The hair, makeup, and costumes bring the characters to life. We found that many cast members enjoy creating their own look. While it is the responsibility of performers to get in touch with the team leaders if they need creative assistance, team leaders should make a point of checking in with each of the acts to make sure they are putting this part of their act together. Team leaders need to know well before "show night" as they will need to find the time to help the performer pull together a costume. While most performers are excited by the prospect of finding a costume, some will overlook details, which the costumer will need to address. ("I think we need to find you something other than sneakers to wear with that tutu.") Some will need to be gently informed of the practical limitations of their costumes. ("Are you going to be able to do a split in that ball gown?") Team leaders must also schedule the appropriate number of helpers for makeup and hair. When the performers participate in the creation of their overall look, it helps them get in touch with their characters. (See appendix A for helpful checklists.)

☆ Costumes ☆

Those who have a flair for fashion and the latest hairstyles and makeup techniques are usually thrilled to be included in a variety show. The word variety says it all. These artists will have a chance to demonstrate their talents in many ways. Costumes can range from very simple to the most elaborate beaded, sparkly evening dresses with headpieces to match—all in the same show. Because each act is totally different, those in charge of designing costumes can be as creative as they care to be, or as conservative as they like.

When working with a group of dancing girls wearing flashy outfits, the costume designer can really use her talent to help create unique, memorable outfits. She is almost like a bridesmaid consultant because the group will be dressed in identical costumes, but their bodies are far from identical! One dancer might want a longer skirt to cover her thighs, another will want higher heels on her shoes, still another will think she needs a brighter color next to her face. The costume designer becomes a consultant, a consoler, and a confidante.

Those responsible for costumes should probably have portable sewing machines, as they will be traveling from group to group designing, altering, and transforming ordinary sheets, curtains, and tablecloths into fantastic garments. They take their sewing kits filled with pins, tape measures, needles, and thread from place to place as they use their incredible imaginations to create magic on the stage.

The costume crew is able to develop something from nothing. A simple feather boa or just the ideal fedora can make a character come alive onstage. Most costume designers have boxes of vests, skirts, aprons, hats, jewelry, headpieces, boots, shoes, dresses, pants, shirts, and uniforms from which to choose. It is seldom necessary to purchase a costume for a variety show as part of the fun is creating your own special look with the help of an experienced costume designer.

Peacocks

We needed a peacock and we didn't happen to have a peacock costume on Orcas Island. We put our heads together and Colleen said, "I live next door to a couple that raises peacocks, let's create our own costume." So off we went in search of peacock feathers. Good news, the peacocks wandered onto our land and left their feathers behind for us to collect.

The building of the bird began when we assembled the following parts of the costume: one black, head-to-toe leotard; one pair of black shoes; one twelve-inch, rectangular, corrugated (with holes) cardboard, painted black; and one piece of double-sided, hook-and-latch tape sewn onto the black body suit and glued just below the waist (on the backside) to the black cardboard. A bunch of precious peacock feathers gently inserted into the corrugated cardboard holes in a fan shape. The peacock person's hair is styled in an upsweep and then sprinkled with color glitter throughout the hair. Have your makeup artist go to town, explore all possibilities, and be creative with the peacock person's makeup. This is an example of making a silk purse out of a sow's ear!

Now the building of the bird is complete and as you can see, a little creativity and your available resources can meet any costume challenge.

☆ In the Dressing Room ☆

The costume group will need plenty of hangers and clothes and shoe racks so costumes and shoes won't end up on the floor and get trampled. Each costume has to be hung and labeled in the order in which the participants will appear onstage. The cast members have to know exactly where their costumes are hung and have all accessories in a plastic bag. These must be returned as soon as the performance is over and replaced in order so there will be no scurrying around before the next rehearsal or show.

Makeup artists relish the thought of being turned loose to transform an ordinary face into a geisha girl, a hobo, or a clown. Most will have their own makeup kits including several different shades of foundation, lipstick, mascara, and eyebrow pencils. The kit will have sponges, powder puffs, powder, adhesive glue, false eyelashes, mustaches, beards, and plenty of cleansing cream and tissue.

When doing makeup for a variety show, several stations should be set up to accommodate four or five characters at once. Characters in the first half of the show should be made up first with the others waiting until later. Stage makeup has to be more exaggerated than street makeup with the eyes and lips becoming the most important focal points. Huge, fluttery eyelashes and bright red lips emphasize the character's expression onstage.

Yes, even the men should wear stage makeup as lip color will make it easier for the audience to understand the character's lines and heavily lined eyes and eyebrows make faces radiant with expression. Powder is necessary so faces won't be shiny. The stage lights tend to drain color from an unmade-up face, so makeup assures that the audience will be able to get the full impact of the character's personality onstage.

Makeup artists prepare the face by cleansing it thoroughly. A basic foundation is applied first, then darker or lighter shades are used to emphasize cheekbones, brows, age lines, under-eye bags, and jowls. Then rouge or blush is used to accent the hollows of the cheeks and to add interest. Most makeup artists apply a red dot at the inside corner of each eye to brighten the whites of the eyes. Lipstick is used on both males and females and the artist generally uses two or three shades of lipstick on one person.

Eyebrows are emphasized with black or brown eyebrow pencils. A skilled makeup artist can transform the age of a face through the use of contours and shading, or alter the features by using prosthetics or sculpting. After all makeup has been applied and the character comes to life, a powder puff or sponge is used to apply translucent powder to "set" the makeup.

Facial hair can be added by using the traditional, theatrical makeup materials: crepe wool and adhesive. This is a rather complicated process as crepe wool comes in braids and must be opened, separated, and applied with spirit gum or adhesive. Use barber shears to trim the facial hair to shape and press with a cloth such as a handkerchief to make it stay in place. Nowadays there is a lot of inexpensive fake hair for sale, and you might be able to create mustaches and sideburns out of products found in the hair care aisle of a discount drugstore or in a beauty supply store. If your makeup artists are inexperienced, it is probably wise to go to a costume or party shop and purchase fake beards and mustaches. There are many of these stores open year round, not simply during Halloween season, so it's easy to purchase just the right facial hair needed for each character. Since many in your cast will be onstage for the first time, we found the fewer additions to worry about, the better. From a distance, beards scratched on with eyebrow pencils work fine.

Be aware of allergies as some makeup adhesives could cause an allergic reaction. Stop immediately and choose a simpler way to add facial hair or leave the face bare and let the character act the part!

If you include the Tummy Act in your show, the makeup artist has a fun challenge making men's torsos look like faces. This creates hilarity and camaraderie backstage as each tummy is displayed for all to see.

Makeup artists know they have to have sponges, brushes, and powder, but often fail to bring enough cleanser and tissue. Be sure to have plenty of these items on hand and purchase more than you think you will possibly use as it goes quickly. Most of the supplies have to be replenished after the dress rehearsal and opening night, so check to make sure you have enough of everything for each show.

Hairdressers also have to be assigned several stations, as many actors require wigs, hairpieces, braids, and elaborate hairstyles. The makeup artists and hairdressers work side by side so they can share supplies and offer creative suggestions to one another.

Some of your hairdressers will be professionals and others will be people who love to work with wigs, create new and different hairstyles, and simply have a knack for working with hair. The professionals will have all the supplies necessary and will bring those with them to the dress rehearsal and performances. They will have combs, brushes, curling irons, hair spray, pins, and accessories. If the makeup artists and hairdressers need additional supplies, these can be purchased for a nominal fee at the pharmacy or donated by people who have worked for cosmetic companies such as an Avon representative or someone who sells Mary Kay products may have free samples they would like to contribute. Our local pharmacy donated a huge boxful of lipstick, rouge, powder, eye shadow, and foundation that was slated to be placed on the sales rack the following week.

☆ Don't Look Down on Hand-Me-Downs ☆

Sometimes professional theaters or local college theater departments are willing to donate costumes. A community theater in upstate New York wanted to set its performance in the 1890s, but had no budget for costumes. A local college had just completed a production of *The Importance of Being Ernest*, for which its costume shop had built a complete wardrobe of authentic clothing for all the characters. One of the cast members of the community theater was friendly with a theater professor at the college. Because the college was on hiatus, the professor felt that he could let the theater borrow whatever its actors could fit into. All the leads in the show ended up wearing beautiful, authentic-looking period clothes. Don't be afraid to ask.

2

GETTING READY

·

CHAPTER 14

Auditions and Casting for a Variety Show, Scripted Play, or Musical

There are several advantages to presenting a variety show as opposed to using a script or putting on a talent show. Although entertaining, a talent show requires minimum time and effort. A group sets up a time, date, and venue (usually the school gymnasium). They advertise by flyers, word of mouth, or newsletter and take all comers. Someone is chosen as master of ceremonies to announce the acts. Each act provides the music, props, or simple sets needed. The curtain goes up, the performers perform, and at the very end, the first, second and third place winners are chosen by audience applause or by the votes of a panel of judges. Generally, ribbons or inexpensive trophies are presented and it's all over. If a small fee was collected at the door, some money is donated to a worthy cause.

The variety show goes far beyond the simple talent show. It is scripted, acts are screened, proper lighting and sound are added, a stage manager keeps everything flowing, the co-directors oversee the entire project, and QUALITY is prevalent in every aspect of the show.

☆ Stories from the Stage ☆

I was directing a skit for a conference. It was "This is Your Life," based on the fifties television show of the same name. I had deliberately designed many of the lines to be delivered from backstage as characters were to be surprise guests. I also took into consideration that the actors would have fewer lines to learn. Everything was going smoothly and the two people who were not able to attend rehearsal were directed by telephone. Yes, telephone!

I was in the car on the way to the conference with one of the phone actors. She announced that she had severely impaired vision and would be unable to read backstage. After recovering from the shock, the driver, whose lines were to be delivered onstage, offered to trade places with her. We immediately began rehearsing in the car. Fortunately, our vision-impaired friend was a quick study and had no problems learning the lines.

We arrived at the seminar and set up for rehearsal. Our other phone actor wasn't there. Someone said, 'He isn't coming until tomorrow!' That meant we had to find another actor. We began rehearsal, and one of the actors, waiting to go onstage, went over to registration and asked if any of the men would like to be in the play. Someone looked interested and she grabbed him and brought him back. He fit in just fine.

That evening, much to our surprise, he arrived in costume and was hysterically funny. He brought down the house. The other phone actor arrived the following evening in plenty of time to watch the play!

—Patricia Williamson, writer and director, Bothell, Washington

☆ Another Story from the Stage ☆

My husband and I supported our community theater and attended auditions to offer encouragement. One night, the director asked if I would fill in and read some lines. I agreed and was shocked when I saw my name posted on the cast list the next day. I protested, "But I'm as green as grass. I've never been onstage before!" In a raspy voice, the director replied, "Don't worry about it. That means I can MOLD you into what I want!" I took the part and have been acting ever since.

—Anne Byrom, box office manager, West T. Hill Community Theatre, Danville, Kentucky

☆ What We Did ☆

We wanted a show that would appeal to the community, have lots of laughs, and one where everyone would have some fun. We all had kids in school so we knew what was popular, and we knew what the "folks" would like. We started there, and put together acts that would appeal to a wide range of our friends. Slapstick or pop songs, everything was in our radar. We searched for many acts, but we looked at more. As people suggested acts, we asked to see them perform, made suggestions, and decided whether or not the act would be appropriate. If not, these people were asked to do other jobs. We liked to keep our shows at fifteen acts with commercials and an intermission, so no one felt slighted if there simply wasn't room for another gymnast or western duo act. The first year we just set up a time to meet at the school to see the performers. If they made us happy and fit into the theme, they were in.

☆ What We Learned ☆

In casting a variety show, we use the same principle we used in casting the annual fourth grade play. We search around and see who looks the part physically. We make sure each child has a speaking part if they so desire and if they are reluctant to be onstage, we give them another job, but everyone must be involved in some way. After we physically cast the parts, we talk with the children and see if they are eager to play that particular character and if the answer is yes, we continue. If not, we make adjustments.

In casting the variety show, we look for people who physically resemble famous people we are planning to portray, ask them to be involved, see if they are able to sing or dance well enough to be coached. Sometimes, a person or small group approaches us with an idea for an act. We listen, watch them perform—either in a set audition or informally—and make the decision as to how they sound, how the act fits into the overall theme, and let them know as soon as possible if they will be included. If the act doesn't fit, we tell them we will save the idea until another year, but in the meantime, we jointly decide on another area in which they can be involved. Very seldom do we have actual auditions where everyone shows up with an idea for an act. We have tried it a couple of times and it just doesn't work for us.

The organically produced show fits better with our philosophy. As with children, we are trying to build self-esteem, create a feeling of inclusion, give the actors a chance to discover their hidden talents and make the show a dynamite production. All of these things combined have worked well for us, but the approach to casting has to be the co-directors choice. Some may feel more comfortable with auditions, while others will want to work as we do—by heart and by feelings and a good match with the theme of the show. We also try to "balance" the range and types of acts so we don't have four acts singing oldies. We think our way works best for us because of our personalities and our goals. But depending upon the kind of organization that is putting on the show, and the type of surrounding community, you may find that auditions are a necessity, in order to get enough people involved, and to ensure the show's balance. We'll tell you how to set up an audition situation a bit later.

☆ Casting the Ensemble ☆

We aren't simply out to do a fundraiser. We want to raise funds, but the intangible benefits are just as important to us as the fundraiser. With this attitude, we have produced almost a dozen shows and all of our goals have been realized every single time. Again, the co-directors have to know themselves and be able to pick and choose ideas from this book that work for them and modify when necessary. Be aware of the fact that the better the show you do this year, the better the audience will be next year.

For us, this has always referred to more than just the actor. "Casting" also referred to picking the best stage manager, set designer, costume designer, and crews. And it didn't stop there. Casting the right people to handle publicity, the box office, and possibly refreshments also played an important part. We looked for the talent in these people the same way we did the performers. Who best fits these roles? How will they add to the success of the production? Is this the right ensemble?

The whole crew that we involve in a play or project knows we value their contribution. We know our strengths and weaknesses, and for a play or other project to succeed, we are willing to let others make their much-needed contributions. The results are worth it.

If you choose to cast using our inclusive, organic method, you will find that once you've convinced a few community fixtures to join in, like our Sha Na Na guys, it gets easier to keep the ball rolling. As soon as a few people get on board you can say, "Did you know a couple guys from the road crew are going to be in it?" That encourages someone who is a bit hesitant to agree to participate. When we told them one of the local musicians was willing to coach them they were eager to come on board.

If you know someone in the community with a special talent you can design an act for that person. If you have a talent slot you'd like to fill, you might want to go ahead and have a more formal audition.

☆ Holding Auditions ☆

You can put a small ad in the local paper asking for interested parties to audition for our show. Some local papers have community calendars that will list auditions. Advertise in the church bulletin or your organization newsletter. Put an article in about the upcoming show and announce audition times. Also, invite anyone who has a talent they would like to showcase in the show or who is interested in working backstage or volunteer in any way. In a small community with a large cast, just about every club and organization will be covered. You will be surprised at how many show up.

Before you run your ad or put up your notice, you need to arrange the date and time, and rent space if necessary. Your notice should contain the time and place of the audition, what kind of acts you are looking for, and how much time each act will have to audition. It should also have a callback number in case people have any questions and so that you can get a sense of how many people are going to show. The co-directors, stage manager, music director, accompanist, and choreographer (if you have one) should be present at the audition if it is possible. You might want to create contact information sheets for your auditioners, where they can fill in their vitals (name, address, phone number, e-mail), and their availability and areas of interest. This could prove useful in widening your pool of volunteers.

When planning the audition, you need to decide if this is going to be a group audition, where everyone sits in one space and watches each other perform, or if it is going to be a closed audition, where each act shows its work to only the production team. A group audition fosters a more "ensemble-like" feeling, but size and layout of your space may dictate the form of your audition.

A sign-in sheet will help you treat your prospective acts fairly—first come, first served. Invite each act, one at a time, to come into the performing space. Greet them warmly and collect the contact sheets. Give them a moment to set up any props or sound. A boom box that plays CDs or tapes should be available, even if you also have a pianist, because not everyone will bring music in the same format. Ask them what they plan to perform. They should begin their act when ready. If there are lots of acts in attendance, you will have to make sure that they don't exceed their time slot—your stage manager can keep her eye on the clock. When the act is completed, say an encouraging word or two to the performers, and let them know that you will call them (give them a parameter—like in a day or two—and try to stick to it).

After all of the acts have gone through this process, you and your team should discuss the acts. There are probably some acts that everyone agrees are surefire. What about acts that show promise? Is there a consensus about that? Are there people that you'd like to use in a different context? ("Didn't think much of her Cher, but I bet she'd make a great Beyoncé.") Check the contact sheets. If someone listed "lighting" as an additional area of interest, and his magic tricks seemed just a bit rusty, maybe he would be better starting out on the tech side.

You and your auditioning team need to hash out these issues. The co-directors have final say, of course, but pay attention to the opinions of the other members of your team. They are the experts when it comes to music and dancing, after all.

Then, as promised, you are going to have to call all of your auditioners. Congratulate everyone, and inform people whether their acts are in or whether you'd like to use their talents elsewhere this year. A word to the wise, though—you have to be very sensitive when you proffer suggestions like this. When a person performs on the stage, he is putting himself into a really vulnerable position. You're trying to build a pool of willing volunteers here, not alienate people.

You may never audition people in this formal manner. You might be all inclusive like we are; you might invite friends of friends to come audition informally in your living room, you might go to local talent shows, and cull your talent from that pool, or you might use some mixture of methods. It depends on your needs and your philosophy.

☆ Casting for a Scripted Play or Musical ☆

Let's assume you have chosen your play or musical, the theater is available for your chosen dates, you're confident that you'll get the sound and lighting instruments you need, and it is time to choose the cast members. Established theater groups have a cadre of people who have worked together in several productions and the co-directors know most of the players. The cast will be selected from this core group with the others taking over backstage duties, publicity, ticket sales, and all of the behind the scenes jobs that are not as flashy, but are equally important. Even if you're new to this, you probably plan on using some actors you already know. If the co-directors want to search for some new actors to become involved, audition information will be announced through flyers, newsletters, newspaper ads, and word of mouth.

An initial audition for a scripted play is similar to an audition for a variety show. We offer some variations in how to run an audition here, so that you can choose the form that seems most workable to you. Potential cast members should be told exactly what is expected of them before they appear for the audition. That information should be included in all announcements. If the co-directors, and the music director and choreographer, want to hear a song or see a dance routine, those auditioning must know this in advance and come prepared.

The co-directors can begin making notes before the formal auditions begin. Watch how the actors arrive in the studio. Are they standing tall? Slumping? Do they exude energy? Do they interact with others or stand to the side? In choosing a cast, it is important to remember this is an ensemble and everyone has to pull together to make everything work. Divas and whiners do not add to the enjoyment of the experience of anyone—especially the directors!

When it is time to begin auditions, the co-directors should start on time and ask everyone to be seated. They thank everyone for showing an interest in the project. Since this will be a fundraiser, the cast and crew will most likely be volunteers. After the introductory speech in which everyone is put at ease, a clear statement of the purpose of the fundraiser is given. Is it to pay those involved in this particular theater? Is it to raise money to renovate or even construct a new building? These goals must be clear to everyone at the audition.

Many co-directors like to have the singing auditions first if they are producing a musical, as this seems to alleviate tension and nervousness on the parts of those who want to land a role in the production. A piano with a competent pianist must be on site so the actors can present themselves at their best. Drawing numbers for the order the actors audition in can make things run smoothly. If the show is to be a musical, those trying out should also have a short dance routine prepared. Perhaps the song and dance could be done as one act or the person could sing a song, then present their talents as a dancer. Alternately, the choreographer might teach everyone a short dance routine, and then watch them in groups, to see how well they picked it up.

The co-directors take notes during this process and realize they are choosing people they will be working with closely for the next few months. The final selection should include people who are enthusiastic, talented, flexible, reliable, and able to work well with the directors, cast and crew. If the selection is a scripted play with no musical numbers, the auditions will change somewhat.

Auditions for a scripted play can be held in one of two ways. One is to have those auditioning bring a monologue or original reading to use as their own, prepared audition material. There are many, many books of monologues and scenes out there—for men, for women, for kids, scenes for two women, and scenes for two men. (See the "Recommended Reading," appendix D, for some suggestions.)

Personally, we prefer the method of having the potential actors use the chosen script for their monologue or scene. The co-directors might decide to photocopy "sides" from the script—that is, short scenes that showcase the characters they are trying to cast. They could choose actors who seemed like the right type for each of the roles in the scene, and then ask them to study the material for a few minutes, and then read it out loud. They could give the actors some direction and ask them to read it again. They might try different pairings of actors.

Or, in the case of a well-known, easily available play, they might ask each actor to prepare a short speech for the character he or she wanted to audition for. Or, perhaps, instead of asking the actors to read, they would set up some sort of an improvisation, so that they could watch the actors interacting with each other, while playing characters. This gives the co-director a feel for which actors would be the perfect match for each part.

As those onstage are auditioning, the co-directors will be taking copious notes to be referred to in private after the last person has exited the stage. The co-directors might want to have two or three others involved in this process as it is so crucial to the success of the show.

The best time to select the cast members is immediately following the audition. If everyone is just too tired to think clearly, schedule a time the following day to discuss, agree, disagree, and become a "jury" to make a final decision as to who will be on the cast list. Waiting three or more days only postpones the inevitable and is inconsiderate to those who have auditioned. They are anxious and are often waiting by the telephone to "get the call" so they can begin planning for rehearsals or start looking for another job. This is true for both paid and unpaid actors. If they are volunteers who are willing to spend countless hours to present a quality show and help others at the same time, they should be shown respect. Their time and feelings are important and as co-directors, you want a cohesive group of happy people so the experience will be both fun and profitable.

☆ Be Prepared! ☆

If you've decided to direct a scripted play, and this is your first time, you may want more advice than the scope of this book is able to offer. See appendix D for some books that can offer you guidance. Inexperienced co-directors who make the decision to use a script should proceed with caution and go to an expert in the community theater, college, or university drama department or get help from people who have more training than the average person has at his or her fingertips.

CHAPTER 15

Selecting, Sequencing, and Timing Acts

After you have a list of acts, sequencing them is the next critical step. The key acts in your sequence are the opening of the show, closing before intermission, opening the second act, and, of course, the final act. Avoid having too many musical renditions in a clump and intersperse these with novelty acts, skits, or commercials. The lineup of acts is paramount to building the total mood for the show. As rehearsals progress, you will know the ones that will bring down the house, fill their eyes with tears, or have them dancing in the aisles.

☆ Stories from the Stage ☆

"I hear the train a comin'
It's rollin' 'round the bend"

Cornerstone Theater was touring the Midwest with a special adaptation of a Shakespeare play we called The Winter's Tale: An Interstate Adventure. The tour bus and equipment truck rolled into Marmarth, North Dakota, and I checked with the site manager to determine where we should set up our portable stage and bleachers. He indicated the far end of the main street, "just this side of the railroad tracks." It looked perfect.

The audience was seated and the performance was underway. The production called for an old clunker of a car onstage and since we didn't want to haul a car around, someone in town always provided one. I drove the clunker onstage, exited the car, and, at that moment, heard a train whistle announcing its imminent approach.

I was dressed as a clown and immediately thought, "Clown it up for a few minutes with my two cohorts onstage, and the train will pass." The locomotive approached and drowned out all sound, as did the following cars. We mimed for a while, and soon realized something else had to be done.

I climbed onto the hood of the car, peered down the track, and saw nothing but railroad cars in the distance. I turned to the audience with a "No hope" clown shrug, and slowly clown-clawed my way to the roof of the car hoping for a better view and playing for as much time as possible. I looked down the track and saw nothing but railroad cars. I gulped for real, repeated my dramatic "No hope" gesture, and hopped from the top of the car to the stage. My partners and I "filled" for a full twenty minutes until the train finally passed.

The town members, having known all along that the train comes through at this time everyday, took it a lot better than we did.

—Christopher Liam Moore, actor, director, and founding member,
Cornerstone Theater Company, Los Angeles

☆ **What We Did** ☆

All acts we auditioned were included some way or another, and written into the script. However, we ran up against a couple of prima donnas who did not want to audition, but insisted on participating based on their experience and reputation. We followed our basic philosophy of inclusion. In both instances, we regretted our decision and the second year we insisted on seeing everyone who wanted to be included.

☆ **What We Learned** ☆

After completing auditions, you have a good idea where you're headed, which acts will fit the theme, and you are fairly clear on the acts you have chosen. To select the acts, look at all the choices and realize you may not use everything. Some tough decisions will have to be made. Possibly you're heavy in one area, such as singers, and light in another. In one instance, we had three groups who wanted to do a country/western duo. Our solution was to combine them into a group of six and it was a great addition to the lineup. Another case involved a woman who wanted to sing a solo, but we already had several musical acts. We asked if she had another way to be involved and together, we decided she would be the person who held up signs designating Act One, Act Two, Intermission, and The End. She was happy to be included and understood our reasons for the final decision.

This is a variety show, so we suggest you include something for everyone. Consider the ages of those in your audience. We created shows that included something for every age group. We cast children as young as five and our oldest performer was in his eighties.

Each age group should present material appropriate for its peers in the audience. A Senior Center may do a show that focuses on World War II music with a walk down memory lane for adults only. If your organization is made up of young and middle-aged people, you want to focus on popular music and commercials of the present day. (See appendix A for a helpful list of tips.)

☆ Make It Timely ☆

In selecting the acts, focus on length of time for each act, as some may need to be extended or shortened. As co-directors, it is your responsibility to tell each act what they need to do to fit into the time structure. This can be addressed in auditions and final decisions will be made after the co-directors have had an opportunity to attend the first rehearsals. For instance, when the Sha Na Na group sang "Runaround Sue" the first year, it was clear the audience was clamoring for more. The following year, Sha Na Na returned with a medley of three songs.

Skits, as all acts, must be tight and pointed so they don't run too long. You may have writers to revise and edit so the acts will be crisp and hold the attention of the audience.

The show should be no longer than two hours, including intermission, so determine how many acts you need based on the length of each act. Usually, that requires around fifteen acts if you include a few commercials and a running dialogue. Factor in time for moving sets, positioning microphones, and applause. Two hours seems to be the best time frame, as people stay engaged, but aren't looking at the programs to see how much longer they have to sit still. Leave them wanting more.

The opening sets the tone for the show. It should be a grabber. A suggestion is to open with a seasoned singer or singers who have written an upbeat, personalized song for your audience. A local group known by all is a good idea. They will warm up the crowd and get everyone involved from the start. It should be a welcome song, and gives latecomers time to be seated before the master of ceremonies or host comes onstage. If the song is humorous and includes some familiar names, those in the audience will begin with a laugh and feel comfortable. It also eases any stage fright cast members may be experiencing. When the opening song is received with laughter and loud applause, the confidence level builds.

After the opening is a great place for the host to walk onstage, welcome everyone, and begin his monologue. It's fun to have the host banter with one of the musicians or a sidekick. If you are using the Ellen format, she can chat with the disc jockey. If you're using a Johnny Carson format, he will have an Ed McMahon as his co-host. (It's fun to make a play on words and change the names of famous people slightly.) One host delivering the monologue and introducing acts can get boring in a hurry. Scripted banter is lively and keeps things moving. The key word here is "scripted." Never put a host onstage without a well-written script. A host who wants to ad-lib may think his jokes are funny, but generally they aren't. A little improvisation is fine if it works, but the beginning of the show needs to be tight and the script adhered to as it sets expectations for things to come.

The second act might be a female song and dance group dressed in flamboyant (generally short) costumes. By now, you have captured your audience's full attention and so on with the show. Weave an interesting mix throughout the first half. The last act before intermission is the time to hit them with something big. You want the audience to head for the break feeling upbeat, and gather in the foyer with smiles on their faces and words of praise.

After intermission, have something unique. It's time to re-engage the attention of everyone. If you have something for the children like SpongeBob SquarePants or The Fantastic Four, this is a good time for that act. Intersperse commercials and skits throughout the first and second halves and save one of your very best acts for last. The Grand Finale ends the show.

☆ Sample Sequence ☆

Just so you can see how we did it, we're listing the order of the acts from one of our variety shows. We've also included an approximate time for each act, and approximate time for each transition between acts, so that you can see a breakdown.

1.   Singer opens the show with an upbeat, personalized song: Five minutes
2.   Host comes onstage with monologue: Four minutes
3.   Dancing girls in flashy costumes: Four minutes

 4. Transition time: One minute
 5. Gymnasts: Five minutes
 6. Transition time: Thirty seconds
 7. Commercial: Three minutes
 8. Transition time: Thirty seconds
 9. "Dem Bones": Five minutes
10. Host/co-host banter: Three minutes
11. Ballroom dancers: Four minutes
12. Transition time: Thirty seconds
13. Country/Western duo or group: Five minutes
14. Transition time: One minute
15. Commercial: Three minutes
16. Transition time: One minute
17. Sha Na Na: Eight minutes
18. Intermission: Fifteen minutes
19. Children's Act (Kermit the Frog and Big Bird): Five minutes
20. Transition time: One minute
21. Host/co-host banter: Four minutes
22. Jazz combo: Six minutes
23. Transition time: One minute
24. Commercial: One minute
25. Ventriloquist: Four minutes
26. Transition time: One minute
27. Carol Burnett skit: Nine minutes
28. Host/co-host banter: Two minutes
29. Tap dance routine: Five minutes
30. Transition time: Fifteen seconds
31. Stand-up comedy routine: Four minutes
32. Transition time: Thirty seconds
33. Commercial: Four minutes
34. Transition time: One minute
35. Tummies: Seven minutes
36. Grande finale: Five minutes

☆ Leave 'Em Wanting More ☆

To have a truly exciting, exhilarating, successful show that makes your audience leave jubilant, selecting and sequencing is of the utmost importance. Bear in mind that this is not simply a talent show. It is a scripted show with a host, sidekick, commercials, skits, musical numbers, unusual acts, and something for everyone. Therefore, the continuity and scripted material is critical to keeping the audience with you and keeping the heat high throughout the auditorium.

When we did plays with high school students, they would often come offstage after a mediocre performance asking how they did. After a great performance, they would come off saying, "Yeah! We killed 'em." When you "kill 'em," you know it and you don't have to ask.

CHAPTER 16

Rehearsals

Rehearsals have to be scheduled by individual groups and time must be allotted for the co-directors to attend all rehearsals when the groups feel they are ready. Dress rehearsals will include everyone involved in the production.

⭐ Stories from the Stage ⭐

We asked a theater director in Mesa, Arizona, if anything unusual had ever happened to her or her cast during a production. She laughed and replied, "Well, if you consider having your key actor arrested onstage and taken away in handcuffs during dress rehearsal unusual, that happened to me!" They were able to find a replacement at the last minute. Expect the unexpected!

⭐ What We Learned ⭐

One positive aspect of doing a variety show rather than a scripted play or musical is that individual acts can set up their own rehearsal schedules and spaces. They work on their own and the directors can drop in from time to time and check on progress. Each act submits a rehearsal schedule to the co-directors so they can plan times to attend one or two of the individual rehearsals and offer critiques and suggestions. Another advantage is each act can practice in one of the member's home or garage. It allows for various options for rehearsal space.

It is incumbent on each act to secure its own rehearsal site and work on all aspects of the act. It is important they contact the directors when they need help with costumes, charts, or items they can't find. The co-directors meet with them and determine which acts are set and which acts need musical accompaniment or special equipment and make suggestions accordingly. Each group determines how many rehearsals will be needed to perfect their act.

Because everyone had other jobs, most of our groups' rehearsals took place in the evenings and on weekends. We found that for the eight weeks of the rehearsal process, we as co-directors spent almost every evening and most of our weekends traveling from rehearsal to rehearsal. We gave suggestions where needed and found that most acts just needed more time to practice to perfect them. The music director went only to the groups that needed his musicians as accompaniment. The "load in" day when all the equipment was to be available was the day before dress rehearsal. We also had a tech rehearsal that day with the directors, the musical director, and a couple of acts present so lighting and sound could be checked.

☆ The Dress Rehearsal ☆

Everyone knows from the outset that dress rehearsal is mandatory. This is where it all comes together: talent, timing, lighting, sound, costumes, props, makeup, sets, hairdressers, and backstage crew. Prior to dress rehearsal send everyone an e-mail or make a phone call giving time, place, and instructions for the evening. Try to have everything setup as it will be on opening night. It won't be complete, but try. It is also a good idea to have your stage crew arrive an hour early so they can attend to details and technical checks. Until this time, the acts have been rehearsing in isolation. Dress rehearsal is great fun because many of the acts will see each other for the first time. There is a built-in element of surprise and delight as each group performs.

When everyone has arrived, the co-directors ask everyone to be seated so they can address the entire group. It is a good idea to give each person written instructions regarding the rehearsal and details about opening night. Provide the cast and crew with the following information:

- Sequence of acts
- Location of costumes
- Location of makeup and hair stations
- Request for silence backstage
- Importance of tracking props for yourself and others
- Dress rehearsal time (it usually runs late)

- Cast and crew requirement of staying until the end (there may be crucial information that needs to be imparted to all)
- Designated parking for show nights

Beginner's luck got us through the dress rehearsal for our first show without a hitch. It was only during the second show that we found we hadn't done enough work with the technical crew prior to dress rehearsal. We found that some of the lights weren't bright enough, and the sound equipment needed some fine-tuning. Cast members didn't take the dress rehearsal seriously (maybe because it had been so easy the previous year) and felt it would all fall into place. That's why we had to call another dress rehearsal three hours before the curtain rose on opening night.

With the clock ticking, we had to get the spot operators comfortable with their jobs, the lighting cues set, and make the cast members aware of when to be ready to go onstage to perform. From this experience, we learned just how crucial dress rehearsal can be. Some groups might want to have two full dress rehearsals, but we didn't want our cast members to be worn out before opening night. For future performances, we found that one dress rehearsal was enough. We made certain we knew what to expect and were prepared for (almost) everything.

☆ Rehearsing the Scripted Show ☆

Rehearsals for scripted shows are quite different. The cast will be smaller, but will have to attend more rehearsals. The director and the stage manager between them will have to schedule these rehearsals carefully, usually working around people's conflict to create modular rehearsals. They will hold separate rehearsals for the different elements of the play that they are working on: blocking, lines, character, fight choreography and any other aspect that requires rehearsal. Modular rehearsal can also mean that if only two actors are required for a particular scene that needs work, only those people will be called for that rehearsal. Or, if it's time to work on the fight choreography, others can either go home or work on something else in another part of the rehearsal hall. Often, you will have much stricter requirements for props, sets, timing, lighting, and sound. If you are doing a musical, you will have all the above plus special rehearsals for music, choreography, orchestra, and chorus.

It is really beyond the scope of this book to go into detailed description of how to direct a play. Suffice it to say that the more organized you are, and the better you know the play, the better your chances of leading your cast to a successful performance. There are lots of books out there that will help you to become a better director; some are imminently practical and some are highly theoretical. (See appendix D for a few choices of books for directors.)

CHAPTER 17

Children Onstage and Offstage

When you include children, either onstage or off, you must be aware of some of the things that can happen. When you have 500 people in the audience who has paid to see and hear the performance, children can cause some disruptions. What do you do? Remember, it is a community event and you want to include everyone.

✦ Stories from the Stage ✦

When directing the children's Christmas program, I try to find a script (or write one) that will allow us to feature each child who has a speaking part in the play. These are about one minute in length and called "mini-monologues." For the first time ever, I took a chance and gave speaking parts to three-year-olds. The play had storybook characters bringing presents to the Christ child. One of the children played Dorothy from the Wizard of Oz and her gift was her red shoes. In addition to reciting her lines, she improvised a little dance onstage. Another child was Cupid and when she gave Jesus her heart, she did an impromptu ballet. All the children did an incredible job and there wasn't a dry eye in the congregation. I was so pleased that the children felt comfortable enough onstage to add their own special touches that made the whole performance unique and touching.

—Patricia Williamson, writer and director,
Bothell, Washington

☆ **Another Story from the Stage** ☆

I was the child wrangler at the Met for five years, which meant overseeing all child performers who worked there. Much of my job consisted of supervising the children backstage, making sure they kept quiet, didn't play with dangerous props, or miss their entrance cue. Of course sometimes things didn't go smoothly.

One willful little boy punched a little girl onstage during a performance of Philip Glass's The Voyage. *This was hardly the first time he'd misbehaved; at intermission I told him he was fired and sent his understudy out in his place. Then I wondered if I really had the authority to make that call. I sought out the director, and as soon as I mentioned the boy's name and what he'd done, he said, "Yes, fire the little brat."*

On another occasion, in a production of Massenet's opera Manon, *Renee Fleming not only sounded ravishing in her first aria, "Je suis encore tout etourdie" ("I think my head is surely reeling"), she looked the part in an eighteenth-century ensemble, complete with a live Russian wolfhound. Opening night was a triumph, but in subsequent nights there seemed to be an odd, not-quite in-pitch accompaniment to her singing. It turned out that the wolfhound was learning the part and joining in the aria. The dog was also fired. He just couldn't carry a tune.*

—*Katherine Burger, playwright and former child*
wrangler at the Metropolitan Opera,
New York City

☆ **What We Did** ☆

We always put gym mats on the floor in front of the chairs. This allows the youngsters an opportunity to sit with their friends and have a close up view of what is happening onstage and hear cousin Margaret without having to peer around heads to see or hear the action. Children in the audience can be handled by two additional child sitters. Our practice was to have a child sitter on either side of the auditorium seated in chairs with a perfect view of those on the mats. Before the performance, the child sitters gave a brief pep talk about audience manners and conveyed the importance of keeping quiet during the acts, applauding when appropriate, and keeping hands and feet to themselves. Although we never had a problem with misbehavior, it is a concern that should be addressed.

☆ What We Learned ☆

We had the children participating in the second half of the show sit in the audience with their parents and then they would switch places during intermission with those participants of the first half. This kept the number of children backstage smaller and easier to manage. The child sitter has to keep an eye on what is happening onstage as well as backstage so the children can be aware ahead of time that their turn is coming. If they are at all nervous, the child sitter can calm their fears. We found no apprehension in the children we worked with as they were all eager to be onstage and strut their stuff. Children, well prepared and directed, add great interest and talent to a variety show. Most community organizations will want to include children if appropriate.

Obviously, a fifty-five-plus community will not find it as necessary to include children onstage as might a group that specifically supports children. Those who are working to build a center for the arts will be more likely to include children as the center will generally be involved in children's productions, so they need to feel a sense of ownership when the building is eventually completed.

In an adult show, children can be onstage, but should be kept to a minimum, as this is not a production primarily for kids; it is mainly a production for adults. One or two acts involving children will be sufficient and one adult act directed to the children in the audience is quite enough. The youngsters can be included in skits or commercials. They will have a minimum number of lines to learn and still be left with a feeling of inclusion and that they are invested in the overall goal.

☆ The Challenges and Benefits of Working with Children ☆

Having children in a production creates a set of challenges not present when working with adults only. (Adults present their own problems!) Backstage behavior is the biggest concern. Limit the amount of children to around eight or ten. It is imperative backstage noise be kept to a minimum. We always had a child sitter backstage to keep them busy and quiet. This involved providing snacks, games, and quiet activities to keep them occupied.

Unwanted comments or noise from backstage, or from the audience, are distracting to the actors onstage and can ruin an especially poignant moment. We also had the emcee speak directly to the children in the audience during the opening monologue. He expressed his delight in seeing so many young people, assured them they were going to have a good time, and solicited their help in keeping excessive movement and noise out of the auditorium. This gave them a sense of belonging and even appreciation for their support and they always rose to the occasion by being cooperative. The child sitters were an insurance policy, as children don't often realize a live performance, where people have paid to see an uninterrupted presentation, is different from watching a TV show at home, where talking, roughhousing, and raucous laughing is sometimes acceptable.

All of us have been to performances where little ones cause distractions. Plan ahead so this doesn't happen to you. Too many hours of hard work have been put into producing a show such as this and all eyes go to the child instead of the action onstage. Add child sitters or make a brief comment before the show informing parents that their children are certainly welcome, but letting them know the cast and crew need a respectful audience to give them their best efforts.

All of these challenges can be met with planning. We believe the show should be an enjoyable experience for the people onstage and for those in the audience. Of course, if it is a show intended for an adult audience, this problem will probably not arise. However, it is a variety show and children add variety and spontaneity, fill their parents and friends with pride, and can bring so much to the overall show. The children feel invested in the project and will take their parts seriously if they have been properly coached.

ONSTAGE

CHAPTER 18

....

The Big Night

The months of planning and rehearsals have all led up to this moment. Let the show begin! If you have read the "Stories from the Stage," you realize anything can happen. So, take a breath, relax and enjoy the ride. Problems will be solved by a competent crew. As Henslowe said, "It's a mystery."

☆ Stories from the Stage ☆

November 20, 2005 began like any other day at the Queen Creek Performing Arts Center. It was opening night of the center's inaugural season. The house was full of anticipation as well as 700 people of which 400 were season ticket holders. The Best of Andrew Lloyd Webber was the show they had all come to enjoy: An evening of music by one of the greatest composers of our time with a cast of four performers who had starred in national tours of some of Webber's shows.

Halfway through the show, Valerie Perry, who played the lead in the national tour of Evita, *started to sing the beautiful song, "Memory," from* Cats. *At the high point of the song as our local pianist was passionately pounding the keys of our Electric Grand Piano, his pinky hit the Calypso drum key!!! Weber's soaring accompaniment turned to the sound of trashcans being thrown about the stage. This Broadway veteran shrieked in surprise, "Can someone help me?" At that moment a fellow artist calmly came onstage and reset the piano key. In true theater style, Valerie continued the song and was rewarded with a standing ovation.*

On the back wall of the Queen Creek Performing Arts Center is a good-natured quote that sums up the whole experience from this highly talented professional: "Thanks for the Memory. —Valerie Perry" The center then purchased a new grand piano!

—Molly Jacobs and Susie Crossland, Queen Creek Performing Arts Center, Queen Creek, Arizona

☆ What We Did ☆

Electricity is in the air and all the work and anticipation comes down to this moment. The actors are milling around backstage, the band is setting up and all are sharing last minute jitters. The stage manager has to shoo away sons, daughters, and friends. The community is so close, everybody in town feels they should have access to everything. They want to join in and the crew just wants to get to work. Finally, the stage area is cleared. Everybody takes a deep breath.

Around the stage, people check their props, have a last minute consultation with the director, or the sound man, and over in a corner someone reminds a member of the act about a critical "take" or move that has been a problem in rehearsal. The stage manager is getting people into their places. The random notes of the musicians tuning instruments can be heard. Lights go off and on as the board is being checked. Last minute details are being attended to. The prop person is looking for that one missing item.

The doors open and the crowd pours in, searching for special seats in the auditorium. Even though the actors have been asked to stay hidden, they can't resist sneaking a peek through the curtain. The excitement is palpable. Many of the audience members are enthusiastically anticipating seeing their friends on the stage.

Everyone has worked hard the past few months and now the adrenaline is really flowing. Suddenly, it is curtain time. There is one moment when an absolute hush fills the total space. Then, Bang! The curtain opens, the theme song booms out, and the lights go up.

☆ What We Learned ☆

Before the Big Night, each and every volunteer should be given the following information:

- Arrival time and where to meet
- What to wear for identification purposes such as ribbons, name tags, or special vests

- Announce the "go to" person if the co-directors are occupied
- Job descriptions for team leaders

(See appendix A for a helpful list of tips.)

☆ Front of the House ☆

We learned that the big night doesn't begin when the curtain rises. It begins when the first car drives up and the passengers emerge with tickets in hand or money to purchase their tickets. The box office has to be open, with plenty of change and provisions made for those who have purchased advance tickets. Will-call tickets should be in a special envelope.

The ushers and greeters need to be in place to welcome people and answer questions about tickets and seating. The ushers show people to their seats. If you have a house manager, this person should be made aware of the question that may be asked and the answers to those questions, such as, "Where are the bathrooms?" "Where do we put our coats?" or "May we have an aisle seat for our small child?"

If the weather is cold outside, have a place for hats and coats. A coat-check person can take items to hang. She might give out numbered tickets to ensure there are no mix-ups at the end of the evening. For more informal performances, audience members can simply hang their coats on the backs of their chairs.

Back in the kitchen, the people in charge of the concessions for the intermission are mixing punch and putting cookies and cupcakes on serving trays. They need to have their tables set up, the refreshments ready, and the ice on hand to be put into the punch just before intermission. The concession person has to watch the show and consult the printed program to allow ample time to get everything in order.

Some large theaters like Chandler Center for the Arts always has a bar with bartenders available, along with finger foods to be purchased. For a smaller production, free cookies and punch already laid out on tables is probably the easiest, most economical way to go. We sold popcorn at a children's play on one occasion and regretted it afterward. The rustling of the popcorn sacks distracted from the action onstage.

Now is the time you need coordination between the front of the house and the back of the house. As curtain time approaches and it becomes apparent the house is virtually full, the house manager signals the stage manager who then flashes the lights to warn the audience the show is about to begin. If starting time is officially 7:00 P.M., you will have to wait a few minutes before you open the curtain, but it is not advisable to wait around too long for stragglers. Flash the lights as close to the stated time as possible. Wait no longer than five to eight minutes. When the front of the house volunteers have completed their jobs, the lights flash and it's time to begin.

☆ Back of the House ☆

At the same time the front of the house is being readied, those in the back of the house have their own jobs to do. The backstage technical preparations are being made, the musicians are tuning their instruments, the stage manager is reminding each act of their cues, costumes are being adjusted, and the children backstage are engaged in a quiet activity. Usually the stage manager is responsible for keeping everyone informed about how much time they have left. By half an hour before the show, she will be announcing the amount of time left until launch time at least every ten minutes. ("Half hour!" "Twenty minutes!" "Five minutes and holding!," etc.) The cast and crew says "thank you" acknowledging that they've heard this time check.

The audience is seated. The stage manager makes sure that the opening performer is ready. She lets the house manager know it is time to close the doors and warns the light board operator that the house lights need to go out. "Places," she tells the first performer. With quiet excitement, the singer watches from backstage as the lights all fade, and the stage goes to black. She takes her place in the darkness. The stage manager cues the light operator. Suddenly, the first performer is illuminated.

And, it's Show Time!

She steps up and begins to sing the welcoming song tailored to the group. We are on our way. As the acts progress, the cast becomes more and more confident and eager to perform. As each act leaves the stage, they are aglow with success. The audience response is contagious and other acts, standing in line eager to get onstage, high five the act coming off and move quickly out to center stage.

The act immediately before intermission is a showstopper and the audience is left wanting more. During intermission, the cast and crew congratulate one another and celebrate, knowing that they have made a difference in the lives of others and they feel a sense of accomplishment. Many are astounded by their own talent. Some had no idea they would be able to sing or dance onstage and yet the thunderous applause proves they are indeed stars. When you have moved the audience, you know it. You don't ask, "How did we do?" You say, "We nailed it!"

☆ Stories from the Stage ☆

After working for weeks directing Bats in the Belfry, *I was exhausted and quite proud of the work I had done with the high school students. As the young man called each cast member's name and they took their bows, he got to the end and said, "And a special thanks to Brenda Johnson for all the hard work she did with us!" There was another teacher in the school who shared my last name and she got the credit for all the hard work I did. For the second performance, I made sure the student had a huge piece of paper in his hand with the name ALLISON JOHNSON on it. I wanted credit where credit was due!*

—Allison Johnson, high school director, Chicago, Illinois

☆ Grand Finale ☆

After the last act, the grand finale is the unifying part of the evening and a chance for the whole cast and crew to be acknowledged and seen together as a cohesive unit. They have shared their time and energy with the audience and the audience reciprocates with rousing applause and tears of joy. As final bows are taken, a circle of love creates a feeling of oneness. It is like a letter of affection to the audience and they respond in kind.

"We're glad we came."

"We're glad you did."

This is truly an occasion for celebration. All the hard work, time spent, friendships formed, challenges resolved, talents unleashed, and personal growth come together in a culmination of appreciation and gratitude. The cast has given their talent and hard work to the community, and the audience responds in thunderous applause. Each person there truly experienced a heartfelt thanks for being a part of this experience.

The band begins to play the show's musical theme softly in the background as the emcee acknowledges the spirited audience and thanks them for supporting the fundraiser. The emcee calls out all of the backstage crew and recognizes the stage manager by name. Each act is announced in sequence of appearance. With the entire cast onstage, the emcee calls out the co-directors for a final bow. As soon as final bows are taken, the band begins playing the closing song, sung by the entire cast and crew. We chose "Goodnight Sweetheart" as our signature song.

"Good night sweetheart it's time to go.
Sure hope that you enjoyed the show.
We hate to leave you,
But we really must go.
Good night sweetheart, good night." (Repeat)

☆ Stories from the Stage ☆

After completing a great performance of Oliver, *the famished actors went backstage to relax at the cast party. Everyone was looking forward to "food, glorious food." They were greeted with twelve plates of "pigs in blankets" and a few baskets of chips. No one had bothered to organize the dishes being brought to the party, so they feasted on the little piggies and learned they should delegate the food for the party the next time they wanted to celebrate!*

—Annette Fisher, volunteer, Santa Fe, New Mexico

☆ After the Show ☆

Opening night has ended with resounding applause so everyone knows it was a success. The first thing people want to do after the show is greet friends and relatives and receive boundless compliments for a show well done. After about thirty minutes cast members are responsible for going backstage to collect their belongings. Let everybody know beforehand by e-mail so there won't be any confusion about what is expected. Volunteer team leaders should inform members of these expectations the week prior to the show's opening. If there's another show upcoming, everything needs to be put back to where it was at the top of the show, so you can repeat the performance the following evening. If that's the only performance, it's time for strike.

☆ Strike! ☆

After a performance is over, you have to strike. This is not a term referring to labor relations, it means that you have to take down and take out all of the stuff that you brought into the theater, or performance space, and leave it spick-and-span for the next group. You will need a team leader or "strike supervisor" who will oversee the cleanup. If you are renting a professional space, you might be charged if this is not done.

If you rented any sound or lighting equipment, it needs to be disassembled, wrapped and packed neatly, and put into someone's van or car so it can be returned. Furniture needs to be returned. If you built any set pieces, these either need to be put back into storage, or if you have no storage, they must be taken apart and put out with the trash.

Costumes need to be returned. Rented items might need to be laundered or dry cleaned before they can be taken back. The dressing room areas should be gone over thoroughly. Props need to be collected and placed in a designated area, labeled, and returned to the owners. The whole space should be returned to the condition it was in before you arrived.

☆ Cast Party ☆

After the final show comes the cast party. The cast party can be held at several different places: the performance site if space is available, a private home, a community club, or a church facility. You could have a volunteer team assigned to provide food and beverages, or you could ask the cast and crew to bring items potluck-style.

☆ Follow-up ☆

It is important to review the whole project within two weeks, as the information will be fresh in the leaders' minds. The sooner the better. Conduct a debriefing meeting. Ask team leaders to bring notes on what went well and the challenges they found in their particular area. Have flip chart available and select a scribe. Call on each team leader to give a report. When all reports have been completed, one person will be responsible for taking the notes, transcribing them and e-mailing them to co-directors and team leaders.

This is a valuable resource to use as you begin to prepare for your next big show.

As soon as possible, co-directors should meet with the financial director for a complete accounting of the financial statement. Everyone—cast, crew, public—wants to know how much money was made. The financial report is made available to anyone who requests a copy. You could e-mail this information to all parties involved in the project. Combine the financials with a heartfelt "thank you" to the entire team.

Send out a post-show press release, containing this information. Send an article to the local paper, along with a photo, as this creates more publicity for your project.

CHAPTER 19

....

Dinner Theater, Raffles, and Auctions

If you want to add another dimension to your fundraiser, you may want to consider a raffle or live/silent auction. Drawings, raffles, and auctions take lead time as you will need to procure a license from your state and to collect needed items. Raffles, auctions, and drawings will increase your revenue and involve more people from the community, thus creating built in advertising.

☆ Stories from the Stage ☆

Imagine my delight, the first time I was in charge of acquisitions for an auction and raffle, I received a call from a man who said he had a car to donate to our program! I was so excited and told him where the drop-off point was and eagerly awaited the arrival of this great prize. When the car was delivered, Tom, the man in charge of our facility, called me to come see it and there sat a rusty old car that wasn't at all what I had in mind! When we lifted the hood, it came off in our hands! Needless to say, we couldn't use the donation.

I learned a very important lesson: Always specify "new or gently used" when soliciting donations for prizes.

—Colleen Schuerlein, event planner, Portland, Oregon

☆ What We Did ☆

Our experience was with a small community that wanted to help build a community center for the arts. We came up with the idea of putting on a show to help raise money to achieve our goal. We wanted to have fun and include anyone who had a desire to be onstage or work backstage. Everyone involved was a volunteer and costumes were scrounged from closets, old trunks, and attics. If we needed a sofa, chair, or lamp, someone would haul it from home and put it onstage. If we needed a stage built, a couple of carpenters built it and rigged light bulbs in coffee cans for spotlights, and musicians were happy to join in the fun. Tickets were left at local stores and we gave out envelopes with twenty-five tickets to anyone who said they wanted to sell. We got the envelopes back with wadded up bills and loose change, sometimes three days after the show.

But, true to its name, the variety show can be used in a variety of ways and at a variety of fundraising levels.

✰ What We Learned ✰

Today, with government funding and grants being cut, organizations are faced with raising a lot of money to keep programs operating. This means bigger budgets, more planning, up-to-date technology, and more publicity. If you are on a board of a corporation, or in an organization that is large enough to make a commitment to raising $50,000 or more, the variety show is still a perfect event for your group. Modifications and additions to the original how-to concept will be needed, and they can be made.

Colleen has been the event manager for an organization in Portland that has put on events raising thousands of dollars. If your organization plans to have an awesome fundraiser, you already have a board of directors, a staff, and standing committees. The budget will be larger and expenses higher. Think big and don't be afraid to ask. To make a large amount of money, the event will probably be "adults only." If you are planning on serving cocktails or wine, have a no-host (cash) bar, because people going to a formal event may want cocktails or at least wine. (Don't forget the liquor license, if applicable.) Of course, you will need servers and a bar set up with ice, glasses, beverages, napkins, small straws, and mixers. Two or three servers should be adequate. Remember to have change available if you are charging for drinks, but a high-end event might require that you have the cocktails and wine served to the patrons at no charge. Your budget will dictate whether you charge for drinks or make them "on the house." Assess your group to determine how much members will be willing and able to pay for tickets. The minimum should be $50, $100 is the norm, but some groups are able to go up to $1,000 per ticket or even more.

An excellent way to produce the variety show for high-end groups is to have a dinner theater in a ballroom with an adequate stage and movable seating. Donors might be willing to pay a large amount for a ticket if this is the annual event of the organization.

☆ Dinner Theater ☆

A formal dinner theater is one of the best ways to attract an audience. Your audience will be assured of a good meal, and look forward to good entertainment as well. If you choose the dinner theater format, survey the location carefully. The dinner theater format is well suited to a hotel ballroom with a stage. You need plenty of room for tables set an appropriate distance from the stage. Large hotels may be willing to give you a price break or even donate the space—especially if you have a resort/hotel owner in the organization. Search for a location that will give you the best price, has enough space, adequate lighting; one that has a good sound system. If you are unfamiliar with lighting and sound, bring a technician to check it out. We've mentioned Drew Campbell's *Technical Theater for Nontechnical People* before—it is also an excellent resource for event planners who are technically challenged. Don't forget "best price" includes all the extras and amenities you receive. The menu quote needs to be added to the service charges.

Decide on the number of tickets you expect to sell and find an appropriate room with adequate seating. Remind the people you are negotiating with that their business will be highlighted in your publicity campaign. Be prepared to let them know the ways you will promote their business. You can feature them on flyers, in newsletters, press releases and in the program. The site will probably want to cater the dinner as well. This eliminates too many cooks in the kitchen. The events manager of the location or hotel will need to know specifics on date, time, menu, and number of guests. You will probably want to decorate so let him know if you have special requirements.

Although your acts can be rehearsed at offsite locations, your dress rehearsal and technical rehearsal must be held on the actual stage. You need adequate time to set up lighting, sound, and have a run-through of the total performance. Be sure to schedule time with the event coordinator at your venue. If you choose to have a dinner theater, the variety show will be considerably shorter than one done as a standalone event.

☆ **Theme** ☆

During your initial planning stages, decide on a theme for the evening, and all decorations, food, and show acts will reflect this theme. Some choices are *Cabaret*, Western, Hawaiian Getaway, A Trip Down Memory Lane, *Great Gatsby*, Hollywood Highlights, a radio show from the thirties or forties, or a Nautical theme. The possibilities are endless.

Our advice is to steer clear of the fifties theme, as it is so common, and select a theme suitable for the targeted age group. Also, if you have something like Western Night, people might want to come in costume. For a more formal affair, a safer bet would be Hollywood Highlights. If those who love to play dress up want to follow the theme, Hollywood characters would lend a more upscale look than say, a Hawaiian theme.

The stage can be simple with a curtain as a backdrop and minimal props. Especially if your theme is something like Radio Serials, sound effects add to the theatricality. Many CDs now feature various effects such as thunder, rain, doorbells, heavy traffic, and the like. A great source for themes and decorations is *www.stumpsprom.com*. You can browse their Web site, get ideas for a theme, and order virtually anything you need for decorations.

When doing a formal, sit-down dinner theater, all decorations, invitations, and entertainment revolve around a chosen theme and image. If your theme is Hollywood Highlights, members can make all decorations or contact a company that sells party decorations, such as Party City. Many Web sites specialize in decorations for high schools proms. Many cities have production stores that can provide almost anything you dream up. Simply order the huge red and white popcorn boxes, director's clapboards, film decorations, and even a red carpet! Waiters and waitresses can be dressed as ushers or Hollywood stars, the centerpieces could have clapboards surrounded by strips of film and silver ribbon.

As your guests walk through the door, they should feel they are in Hollywood and a searchlight can be stationed out front to add to the feeling of a movie premiere. Your variety show lineup would include songs and dances from movies old and new, or impersonations of famous movie stars quoting well-known lines, adjusted just a bit to include some members of the audience. Anything that can be done to include the audience in the entertainment goes over well as long as it is in good taste and doesn't offend.

People love to see their friends and co-workers in costume onstage. You can watch a hundred movies or TV shows, but nothing makes a lasting impression as much as seeing someone you know performing.

As dessert is being served, or cleared, it is time to begin the variety show. The master of ceremonies opens the show and you're off and running. This version of the variety show will be much shorter than the original version. A forty-five minute, excellent show with a tight, well-written script highlighting people and businesses in the audience will be long enough. There is no need for an intermission and six or seven acts will be sufficient. You might want to have a local commercial or two, but keep the time limit down as people have already been sitting through dinner and a complete show with intermission would be way too much.

☆ Getting Organized ☆

To organize a dinner theater, select a host couple to be responsible for each table of eight. Each host team sells the six remaining places at their table. Prepare a packet for each couple that contains information and tickets. You want your hosts to be able to clearly communicate the purpose of the fundraiser to the prospective ticket purchasers. The host couple pays for their tickets and knows they are making a contribution to the program. This is a commitment that must be met, so be very clear when you are assigning host teams. The intent is to have every seat filled. Your planning team will determine the dinner theater ticket price.

☆ Appetizers and Hors D'oeuvres ☆

Some groups forego the dinner and simply have hors d'oeuvres in the foyer with high tables and tall stools placed around so people can graze and visit. Community theaters and centers usually have a perfect space in their foyer; a large banquet hall would work. Refreshments and drinks will be served in the foyer. If an auction or raffle is planned, items can be displayed in the foyer or in another room. Many local eateries love to participate in "A Taste of . . . " event, for certain causes and particularly if they can attract new customers. This event is one where restaurants bring in samples of their cuisine and a banner is placed across their serving areas, announcing "A Taste of Rigatoni's" or "A Taste of American Grill." Guests are provided with plates, forks and napkins, then wander from booth to booth sampling taquitos, meatballs, Chinese food, or whatever special food the restaurant has to offer. You can offer a prime venue for local restaurants to market their wares and, at the same time, provide excellent food for the audience.

Most community theaters will have stationary seats in the auditorium, so it is not possible to have an entire dinner with tables set up in the theater. Therefore, "fixed seat" venues lend themselves nicely to the hors d'oeuvres and wine scenario.

The Village Theatre in Issaquah, Washington, has a unique way of presenting the upcoming season by inviting the season ticket holders and others who are interested in the arts. Wine companies donate beverages, restaurants offer to provide finger foods, and hotels lend glassware, utensils, and serving dishes. Bar tables are set up in the foyer and people enjoy the cocktail party atmosphere. Then they are ushered into the auditorium for entertainment and a live auction.

The entertainment is a preview of the productions for the upcoming season. It is a great opportunity to showcase talent and to generate enthusiasm. The casts of the new shows perform one number from each production. Every show is represented, which encourages the audience to purchase season tickets. The Village Theater is fortunate in that it can hold events in its own spaces, so planners don't have to search for a place, or buy or rent equipment, as it is all there. They make it clear that the goal is to raise money for the ongoing operation of the two theaters.

☆ Raffles ☆

Since the goal is to raise a lot of money, you will obviously need some high-ticket items for a raffle. You will get more participants since they only have to pay a small amount for a raffle ticket as opposed to paying much more for a diamond ring in a silent auction. Besides, you can sell raffle tickets over a long period of time to a huge audience. Since winners do not have to be present to win, you can entice people who would not be able to attend your fundraiser to purchase tickets. In this way, raffle sales will raise awareness for your group.

One big draw, such as a new car, will increase interest. Tickets generally sell for around $10 each or three for $25. If the car is donated, be sure the car dealership is featured prominently in your flyers, programs, and press releases. It sounds easy to go out and find a dealership to donate a car or a successful builder to donate a new home, but wait! This is far more complicated than it sounds. Give the acquisitions person plenty of lead time. If your group does not have a raffle license, you will need to obtain one. Check with the Department of Justice in your state. In Oregon, we register with the Oregon Department of Justice under Oregon's Charitable Trust and Corporations Act-Gaming Unit. You may choose to go online and do a search for this information in your state. Each state will have a different set of rules to follow for a nonprofit raffle.

If you are fortunate enough to get an expensive, attractive car, display it prominently for a couple of months prior to the event. Shopping malls are often willing to provide space to display the car and sell tickets. They, too, should be included in your promotional materials. Emphasize that winners do not have to be present to win. You can sell tickets weeks in advance to generate publicity and make your fundraiser more lucrative.

If you choose to have a raffle with your show, decide on five fabulous prizes, including the car, a week's vacation to Hawaii with airfare, or jewelry (a diamond or gemstone ring, watch, or another special piece). A motorcycle or dinner for eight prepared by your organization's board will attract a diverse group of members. Make announcements at your school, church, or club that you will be holding a fundraiser and are looking for high-end items. Many people have weekend homes and timeshares they would love to donate. Add this to donated air miles and you have a very attractive holiday package.

Let everyone know the drawing will be held on the night of the dinner theater. This adds a grand element of excitement to your gala event as you can weave the drawings throughout the dinner portion of the evening. Spice it up with a little drum roll! Set up a display the night of the event and sell tickets there. For extra security, you might want to display pictures of the smaller items such as rings or watches. If you set up your ticket sales by the display, it creates energy and excitement about the possibilities of winning. People can buy into the dream of winning if they see the actual prize.

Big-ticket items, such as a vintage car, will be a big draw and your five fabulous prizes will sell many raffle tickets. Don't overlook the contributions that can be made from donations that aren't quite as flashy. Some people come to an event with a set amount of money to spend and are looking for a less expensive way to be included, and to support the cause.

Smaller items can be included in a balloon raffle. Several volunteers dress up to reflect the evening's theme. This adds a festive feeling as they circulate among the crowd carrying bouquets of balloons. These will be reasonably priced, so a credit card machine isn't necessary. The balloon volunteers need pockets or attractive aprons to hold cash and checks. If someone buys a five-dollar balloon, the purchaser pops it and reads what is inside. There is a slip of paper saying either what has been won along with the prize's claim number or "Thank you, try again!" Five or ten dollars per balloon is a good price range and allows for more involvement. Obviously, the ten-dollar balloon prizes will be of higher quality than the five-dollar balloon prizes. To make it really exciting, you could have a few fifty or one hundred dollar balloons, but only if the prize is quite valuable and, of course, no "Thank you, try again!" on the higher priced balloons! The prizes are displayed on a table with their corresponding number and a volunteer gives the winners their prizes when they present a winning slip of paper.

☆ Auctions ☆

If you decide to have a live auction immediately following dinner with a professional auctioneer, this will cut down performance time. Without a live auction, a forty-five minute show would be appropriate. With a live auction, the entertainment should be limited to thirty minutes. Combining a dinner, an auction, and quality entertainment will make the high ticket cost more palatable.

If you decide to host a silent or live auction we recommend tripling the time you think will be needed to generate donations, contact auction donors, pick up the items, store them, create an accurate database of donors, and organize the auction paperwork and/or bid sheets. Collect attractive key auction items in a range of prices early in the event planning process, so these items can be included in the advance publicity for your event. They will generate buzz in the community and help set the tone for the quality and type of subsequent items that are donated.

Some groups combine auctions with raffles. The auction can be silent or live. Be aware that a live auction generates much more enthusiasm and probably will raise more money, but a professional auctioneer will have to be hired or be a volunteer. A professional auctioneer has a rare skill and can generate much more money for your group than an amateur searching around the stage for the next item. If the action isn't kept moving, people lose interest and drift away. Watching a professional auctioneer is almost a show in itself.

☆ Handling Money and Tickets ☆

In the past, people paid cash or wrote checks. Today, practically everything is purchased by credit card. You will lose out on a lot of revenue if you do not have credit card machines available at the ticket sale sites, at the door, by the raffle table or for the live or silent auction. Those machines can be borrowed from local banks or businesses. Thorough instructions on how to work the machines are vital. It is best to have experienced volunteers to work the machines efficiently as long lines turn people away. You could lose hundreds of dollars simply because you forgot to arrange to take credit cards! Since businesses have to pay a fee for credit card transactions, the organization holding the event should be responsible for the fees unless the business owner chooses to pay for the service as part of their contribution to the event.

Be sure you have ample bills and coins. There is nothing worse than having someone ready to make a purchase with a large bill, and you cannot make change. Remember that the banks will be closed by the time your event starts, and you don't want to run down to the Circle K for extra dollar bills. Use standard procedures when you set up any station handling money. Give them a prescribed amount, have them count the "till," and sign for it. At the end of the night, count again, and deduct the original amount in the till and put the net amount on a prepared form. Turn all money and balance forms over to the person in charge.

☆ Helpful Hint ☆

When you put out the call for items, be sure to say new or in perfect condition. You can set up a drop-off point for the items and have someone in charge of that area to determine what gifts will be appropriate and their approximate value. People who donate a prize should give their name, phone number, and address. A letter on organization letterhead is sent out stating the prize donated for tax purposes. Do not assign a value to the donation. The value will be determined by the donor to claim an appropriate deduction. Leftover prizes can be donated to a worthy cause.

☆ Ticket Sales for Auditorium Seating ☆

In most cases, you won't give audience members actual seat assignments, as you would in a Broadway theater or on an airplane. Instead you will have two prices for tickets and two categories of seating: general and preferred. Most traditional theater spaces have automated box office programs. Also, most auditoriums already have numbered seats. You may want to use the numbers that already exist on the theater seats to designate preferred seating, for example, designating all the seats in rows A through J as preferred.

If there is no automated system in place, have the printer create tickets in two different colors. Be certain you are clear on the number of seats available in your venue *before* the tickets are printed.

Go to the site, decide how many seats are to be allocated to preferred seating and work from there. Fifty to seventy-five is a good starting place. Many people will pay extra for up-front seating and like being assured they will have a specific seat, as general seating is first come, first served. It is important the preferred seats are all numbered. If the seats in your auditorium do not already have numbers on them, have the graphic department print numbers on 8 1/2" × 11" sheets of paper and securely tape these numbers to each chair. An even number of seats in each row is preferable for designing the seating chart.

The number on the general ticket is mainly a way to keep track of number of tickets sold. Tickets are sold at local businesses, the board members of your organization can sell tickets in person or online from your Web site. Many people like to have online ticket sales available. You have your hotline already set up. Handing out a packet of tickets to cast and crew members is not advisable, as it is too difficult to keep track of these sales. If you are selling tickets in a group that sells tickets on an ongoing basis such as a church, you will have a ticket sale table located in the lobby. You must have a ticket tracking system. Ours was primitive and based on the trust of a small community. If you need greater security your team leader needs to research ticketing software, or devise a system appropriate to your community and your resources.

While a swanky cocktail party/silent auction in a hotel ballroom may seem a far cry from a humble variety show on a tiny island, as you can see, both require planning, generous donors, and visionary directors. The only difference: your vision must be scaled to how deep your audience's pockets are and how high the contributions bar is set.

CHAPTER 20

....

Curtain Down

Our last story from the stage brings the experience of putting on a show up to date. Recently, a group of creative people on Orcas Island presented *Orcas Idol,* a takeoff of the mega-hit *American Idol,* a television show with millions of viewers. Since the producers of *Orcas Idol* did not have access to a national phone network to collect votes, they used paper ballots, compressed the format, and tallied up the votes while other prescheduled performances entertained the audience.

✰ Stories from the Stage ✰

We began with an announcement so contestants could sign up for auditions and select music that would highlight their voices and talents. We included contact names and phone numbers for those who could not sign up at the indicated time or who needed more information about auditions. We held auditions at the local Grange Hall and tickets sold at the door for $5. Judges had a list of criteria, which they shared with contestants, to evaluate the performances. Eight contestants were chosen and they joined three performers pre-selected in order to generate interest for the event. Eleven contestants participated in the final competition for Orcas Idol.

Our big show was held a couple of weeks later at the Orcas Center with a master of ceremonies and the same panel of judges. Tickets were $15. We asked contestants to choose three songs from different genres; the accompaniment came from our catalog or their own Karaoke CD. Each performer was assigned a number for voting purposes, which remained consistent throughout the show. Our printed program included color-coded ballots and pencils were provided. After the first round of performances, the audience voted for its three favorites, and runners patrolled the aisles to collect the ballots. Ballots were taken to another room where ten counters quickly tallied votes during intermission and narrowed the field to five singers.

After intermission, the five remaining contestants sang a second song. The audience voted for two favorites; ballots were collected and counted. As votes were counted, a student improv group entertained the audience. The top three vote-getters remained and moved on to the final round. The same procedure was used. While a winner was determined, the high school jazz band provided entertainment.

Jenole Peacock, a talented high school senior, won and received a $200 prize plus a recording session at Jim Bredouw's studio. Jim is a well-known producer and founder of The Funhouse. We raised additional funds by taking advance orders for CDs of the night's performance.

We had a lot of fun, involved the whole community, and Orcas Idol raised money for the Orcas Island Prevention Partnership. The show was sponsored by the local Radio Shack and supported by many community-minded island businesses and individuals.

—Jan Wiemeyer, Producer, and Gary Bauder, Vocalist,
Eastsound, Washington

The above information was provided by two islanders keeping the spirit alive and can be used as an outline of sorts for putting on this kind of show. If your group has access to a recording studio, offering the winner the chance to make his or her own CD is a perfect prize. If you are operating on a smaller scale, a cash prize, a trophy, or a gift certificate is great.

✯ The Last Word ✯

We wrote this book (and our Web site, *www.letsputonashowfundraising. com*) with the same passion we had when we produced the variety shows. We said, "Hey, let's put on a show!" and then we said, "Hey, let's write a book about it!" The notes and writing began over twenty years ago. It was put aside as other things filled our lives. Over the years, we kept thinking about it, talking about it, and saying we should get around to it when the time was right. Now, the time is right. People are clamoring for ways to raise funds—from the smallest clubs at the grassroots level to the people who produce plays on and off Broadway.

Most of us are getting tired of reality shows on TV, and reading and hearing the same news about the same celebrities in every book, magazine, and newspaper we pick up. We are eager to get off the couch and go out and create our own entertainment in our own way.

Hopefully, this book will spark your interest and creativity and will be used to contribute to worthy causes (and there are many). You can experience the joy and fulfillment we had when working with our friends and neighbors, enjoying every minute. Good luck and best wishes to you when you put on your own show.

APPENDIXES

....

Contents

⭐ **Appendix C – Rules for Auctions** *181* ⭐

⭐ **Appendix D – Recommended Reading** *185* ⭐

·······························

Tips and Checklists

☆ Qualities of a Good Co-Director ☆

- ➤ Dedicated
- ➤ Enthusiastic
- ➤ Well known and respected in the community or organization
- ➤ Willing to work for the joy of the experience
- ➤ Organized
- ➤ Sensitive, yet able to make tough decisions
- ➤ Able to interact with people from all walks of life
- ➤ Inclusive, rather than exclusive
- ➤ Enjoy meeting new people and doing something different
- ➤ Willing to see problems as challenges, instead of roadblocks
- ➤ Able to delegate responsibilities

☆ Critical Questions to Ask When Seeking a Performance Venue ☆

➤ What type of venue would work best for your show?
(*In what season will your show take place? Could it take place outdoors? In a tent? Do you need a stage? How important is audience comfort?*)

➤ What are the optimal days for the performance(s)?
(*Start planning at least six months in advance, and choose three potential dates, so you have flexibility*)

➤ How many performances?

➤ What is the seating capacity of the potential venue(s)?

➤ What is our budget for space rental?

➤ What is the cost of the potential rental space(s)?

➤ What are the technical capacities of the space?
(*Have your sound and lighting people, and/or the technical director of the space guide you through this one*)

➤ How large is the stage?

➤ Does the venue have other necessary spaces and facilities available? Some common ones include:

- Bandstand
- Restrooms for cast and audience
- Dressing rooms
- Lobby
- Green room
- Hair and makeup stations
- Costume storeroom
- Box office
- Concessions

✫ Tips for Publicizing Your Fundraising Event (Chapter 4) ✫

➤ Agree upon a succinct statement that clearly explains to all how the funds will be used

➤ Print mission statement and other information to be included on all publicity material

➤ Set up meeting with co-directors, publicity teams, and graphic artists

➤ Set up hotline (if applicable)

➤ Create Web site, add capability for online ticket sales if possible

➤ Organize volunteers for online ticket sales (if applicable)

➤ Encourage volunteers to publicize via word of mouth

➤ Create flyers and posters. Post them on applicable spaces like Chamber of Commerce and church bulletins.

➤ Write press releases. Send them to applicable publications like school or church newsletters, magazines, newspapers, and radio and television stations

➤ Brainstorm other ways to publicize the show

➤ Include complimentary tickets in the publicity budget

➤ Distribute tickets for sale

➤ Collect revenue and unsold tickets

➤ Make an accounting of all tickets sold

➤ Arrange to sell tickets at the door if necessary

☆ Tips for Creating a Top-Notch Program (Chapter 5) ☆

The information included in the program will be determined by size, format, and number of pages. Enlist the services of a professional designer, if possible. He or she will be able to work with the limitations of your layout and will be familiar with printing conventions.

➤ If working with an established organization, use its logo or signature image on all printed material
➤ If working solo, create a signature image or logo

Content
➤ **Front cover:**
   • Include the logo or signature image, the show's title, and date of the performance

➤ **Inside cover:**
   • State the producing organization (if applicable), the vision statement, and a "thank-you" section to volunteers

➤ **First page:**
   • Include the show's title, and the names of the co-directors and producers at the top of the page
   • List of acts in first half of show
   • Intermission

➤ **Second page:**
   • List acts in second half of show
   • If space allows, list the names of musicians, the stage manager, writers, and stage crew

➤ **Back cover:**
   • Special acknowledgments, volunteers and donors names (if applicable)
   • Include ads if applicable and if space allows

Printing
➤ The co-directors should proofread program again and again before final printing, taking special care to review the names of volunteers and donors, if listed

☆ Tips for Sets, Props, Lighting, and Sound (Chapter 9) ☆

Sets:
➤ Make a list of sets needed, act by act
➤ Speak to the carpentry team leader regarding what needs to be built, what can be borrowed or bought, and what pieces can be shared by more than one act
➤ Speak to each act about modifying its set pieces to match budget and time constraints of the construction team
➤ Set deadlines for building, borrowing, and transporting set pieces

Props:
➤ Make a list of props needed for each act
➤ Search for unusual props
➤ Have unprocurable props built by the carpenter, lighting, and/or costume crews

Lights and Sound:
➤ Check the lighting and sound equipment and power sources available in space with lighting team leader and sound team leader (or the technical director of the space), and stage manager
➤ Have the stage manager and lighting team leader discuss lighting needs with each act, including spotlights, blacklights, floodlights, reflective lights, etc.
➤ Have lighting designer draw up lighting plot to accommodate needs and budget
➤ Rent lights, cables, etc., to fulfill lighting plot (if applicable)
➤ Have the stage manager, sound team leader, and music director discuss sound needs with each act, including instruments, amplification, standing mikes, body mikes, etc.
➤ Have sound team leader draw up plan to accommodate needs and budget

☆ Tips for Writing Your Own Script (Chapter 10) ☆

➤ Watch comic television shows for inspiration
➤ Keep your eye out for local issues that could be used to personalize your script
➤ Choose a basic format for your script (i.e., *The Ellen DeGeneres Show? Saturday Night Live?*)
➤ Select a team of writers
➤ Schedule writing meetings
➤ Watch popular TV shows and take notes to assist in writing personalized jokes and banter
➤ Write skits
➤ Write commercials
➤ Make suggestions for improvements and changes
➤ Re-write script
➤ Print final script
➤ Rehearse final script before dress rehearsal

☆ Checklist for Wardrobe (Chapter 13) ☆

Obviously, the wardrobe team leader will have to determine what the needs of this particular show are, and modify the checklist so that it reflects those needs. No point in having items on the list that your show doesn't require, or, conversely, not including items that you do need.

❑ Sewing machine
❑ Fabric (list each fabric and amount, needed by each act)
❑ Found items (list items needed by each costumed performer: boas, hats, uniforms, vests)
❑ Thread
❑ Straight pins
❑ Needles
❑ Tape measures
❑ Scissors and pinking shears
❑ Cellophane tape
❑ Duct tape
❑ Masking tape
❑ Jewelry (breakdown, act by act)
❑ Set pieces (material used to dress the set: old sheets, tablecloths, curtains, etc.)
❑ Shoes, boots, slippers (footwear, as needed by each performer)
❑ Clothes racks
❑ Hangers
❑ Shoe compartments
❑ Felt markers to label costumes
❑ Full length mirrors
❑ Plastic bags (for props and accessories)

Responsibilities Before, During, and After the Run of the Show

➤ Make sure each costume piece contains the name of the person who is to wear it. Accessories should be in a bag labeled with that person's name, and hung from the same hanger.
➤ Help performers to make changes during the performance.
➤ Make emergency repairs backstage.
➤ Make sure clean, undamaged costumes are returned to racks before the beginning of the next performance.
➤ Return borrowed costumes and accessories after the show.
➤ Store costumes for next year's performance.

☆ Checklist for Hairdressers (Chapter 13) ☆

This list (and the one for makeup artists on the next page) should contain those items that are applicable to your particular show.

- ❏ Mirrors
- ❏ High stools for hairdressers
- ❏ Large boxes to hold materials
- ❏ Electrical outlets
- ❏ Curling irons
- ❏ Combs
- ❏ Brushes
- ❏ Hand mirrors
- ❏ Hairpins, hair clasps, hair clips
- ❏ Heavy hold hair spray
- ❏ Wigs
- ❏ Brush rollers
- ❏ Hot rollers
- ❏ Pronged hair lifters
- ❏ Hand-held hair dryers

☆ Checklist for Makeup Artists (Chapter 13) ☆

- ❏ Stools for makeup artists
- ❏ Storage containers for makeup
- ❏ Foundation cream in three shades
- ❏ Lipstick in four or five shades
- ❏ Rouge and blush
- ❏ Mascara
- ❏ False eyelashes
- ❏ Adhesive
- ❏ Eyebrow pencils in black and brown
- ❏ Tweezers
- ❏ Crepe wool/fake mustaches, beards and eyebrows
- ❏ Nose putty/latex/prosthesis
- ❏ Makeup sponges and brushes
- ❏ Neutral powder
- ❏ Cleansing cream
- ❏ Tissues
- ❏ Wash cloths
- ❏ Soap
- ❏ Towels

✶ Tips for Selecting, Sequencing, and Timing Acts (Chapter 15) ✶

Timing
➤ Limit show to two hours in length
➤ Each act and the grand finale will probably run about five minutes, though times can vary between three to ten minutes
➤ Commercials should be about three minutes
➤ Transitions (set changes, microphone setups, applause, etc.) will vary from about fifteen seconds to no more than a minute

First Half: Approximately Fifty Minutes
➤ The opening act should be a high-powered musical act that will make the audience feel welcome.
➤ Follow the opening act with the introduction of the host and his sidekick. Give the audience a sense of what they are in for.
➤ Fill in other acts for first half of show. Try to alternate between musical, novelty, and comedy.
➤ Immediately prior to intermission, present a high-energy group with engaging toe-tapping music and wide audience recognition and appeal.

Intermission: Approximately Fifteen Minutes

Second Half: Approximately Fifty Minutes
➤ Begin second half with something for the youngsters. Use an up-to-date musical number including cartoon characters or television favorites for the kids. This will play to the younger set and get everyone back into the action.
➤ Fill in the rest of the second-half acts. Try to alternate between musical, novelty, and comedy.
➤ The closing act could be high-powered and energetic like the "Tummies" act (see page 94) or a solemn and heartfelt slide show (see page 95).
➤ The grand finale is where performers take their bows and special farewell activities take place such as thank yous, a group song, or flower presentations (Make sure the host's list of names for the thanks yous is accurate.)

☆ Tips for the Big Night (Chapter 18) ☆

With all the anticipation and excitement on opening night, it's easy to get nervous or carried away. This list of tips will help you keep track of what needs to happen before the curtain comes up.

Front of House:

- Make sure that the box office staff, ticket takers, and greeters are in place

Stage crew:

- Sweep/mop the stage and clear the house of garbage, personal belongings, etc.
- Set up any scenery that needs to be onstage at the top of the show and ready all other pieces for efficient entrances and exits

Prop crew:

- Set up all necessary props on labeled prop tables, so that performers can easily grab them and return them on the way on and off the stage

Lighting and sound crew:

- Run through an equipment check to make sure everything is in working order
- Let the stage manager know if all is well or if repairs must be made

Costume crew:

- Make sure all costumes are placed where they belong, and that all costumes are in good repair
- Help with dressing and any emergency repairs

Makeup crew:

- Set up stations

Stage manager:

- Check in with performers to make sure that all are present

Performers:

- Get dressed
- Go through makeup
- Locate any special props

➤ After checking with the stage manager, the house manager opens the doors to the auditorium and lets the audience enter.

➤ Stage manager cues "pre-show" music, if there is any.

➤ Accompanist and any musicians set up their instruments and tune up.

➤ Stage manager keeps performers informed as to how much time is left until curtain.

➤ Stage manager and house manager confer about whether the audience is in, and whether everything is set up backstage.

➤ House manager closes the doors.

➤ Stage manager cues house lights out, stage lights up, and the show begins!

APPENDIX B

Sample Forms

☆ Production Schedule ☆

This calendar is a sample of what we did between November and February.

Week of	Task
November 20	➤ Co-directors meet
	➤ Finalize decision to "put on a show"
	➤ Choose possible dates for performance
	➤ Print mission statement and reason for fundraiser
	➤ Choose theme for show
	➤ Start search for insurance agent, attorney, and CPA
	➤ Create a budget
	➤ Begin looking for an appropriate venue
	➤ Start thinking of possible acts
	➤ Find and meet with graphic designer for publicity materials
November 27	➤ Inform people that a show is being planned as a fundraiser
	➤ Contact possible team leaders and ask them to begin assembling crews
December 4	➤ Invite sound, lighting, and construction team leaders to accompany co-directors to survey venues
	➤ Select musical director and find musicians
	➤ Finalize dates and venue

	➤ Begin asking people to participate as onstage performers
	➤ Schedule and advertise auditions if necessary
December 11	➤ Choose stage manager
	➤ Assemble backstage crew
	➤ Conduct auditions
	➤ Notify performers of casting choices
	➤ Begin research on royalties and contact ASCAP
	➤ Ask participants to use the remainder of the month to think about their acts and/or their roles in the production
	➤ Schedule team leader meeting for January
	ENJOY THE HOLIDAYS!
January 2	TIME TO GET DOWN TO BUSINESS!
	➤ Conduct team leader meeting
	➤ Begin creating script
	➤ Individual acts gather to rehearse
	➤ Co-directors take lighting, sound, and construction crew to the chosen venue again to assess "final" needs
	➤ Lighting, sound, and construction crews plan what is needed
	➤ Acquire items for raffles or auctions if applicable
January 9	➤ Graphic artists design flyers, posters, and programs
	➤ Purchase tickets to sell
	➤ Begin search for costumes, props, music
	➤ Prepare recorded music
	➤ Give list of music needed along with musical charts and CDs to music director
	➤ Co-directors attend individual rehearsals and make suggestions for improvements
	➤ Set up public service announcements with radio and TV stations
	➤ Check with team leaders to see if additional volunteers are needed
January 23	➤ Print flyers and posters
	➤ Keep in contact with team leaders
	➤ Follow up on problems to be solved

January 30	➤	Distribute flyers and posters
	➤	Begin construction of sets and backdrops
	➤	Start ticket sales
	➤	Continue visiting rehearsal sites
	➤	Begin securing costumes
	➤	Send cast members in costume to service organizations to promote show
	➤	Check on sets and backdrops
	➤	Construct stage or rent tent if necessary
	➤	Search for props
	➤	Send press release to local newspapers
	➤	Assemble makeup and accessories
February 20	➤	Sequence acts
	➤	Continue to supervise individual rehearsals
	➤	Disseminate written information announcing date and time for dress rehearsal
	➤	Send program to printer
	➤	Make arrangements for concessions and servers
	➤	Give final instructions to ushers and box office volunteers
	➤	Organize cleanup crew
	➤	Borrow or rent credit card machine
February 24	➤	Load in equipment
	➤	Tech rehearsal
February 25	➤	Full dress rehearsal
February 26	➤	Opening Night!

☆ Team Leader Contact Sheet ☆

Team	Leader's Name	Phone Number	E-mail Address	Street Address
Carpenters				
Cast Party				
Child Sitters				
Cleanup				
Database				
Finances				
Graphic Design				
Greeters				
Hairdressers				
Lighting				
Makeup				
Moving Crew				
Music				
Props				
Publicity				
Sound				
Stage Crew				
Stage Manager				
Ticket Sales				
Wardrobe				
Writers				

☆ Outline for First Meeting with Team Leaders ☆

Team Leaders Meeting, to be held on _____

I. Welcome volunteers and thank them for their commitment to the project
II. Explain purpose for the fundraiser
III. Distribute notebooks for each team leader that contain:
    A. Page 1: Vision statement, mission statement, sponsoring organization, and gratitude note from the co-directors
    B. Page 2: Job description for each team
    C. Tab One: Team leaders and directors contact sheet (as completed up to this point, if information is to be added, a new sheet will created by co-directors)
    D. Tab Two: Team members contact sheet (as completed up to this point, revised sheets will be distributed by co-directors)
    E. Tab Three: Meeting and rehearsal schedules (could be production schedule or a modified version thereof)
    F. Tab Four: Expense sheets with pockets for receipts
IV. All team leaders check master copy of contact list for errors. Sign off or mark corrections
V. Solicit ideas from leaders
VI. Collect information on people who are interested or potential participants
VII. Recruitment of team members by each team leader
VII. Collect any ideas for production and talent
VIII. Goals for next meeting for each leader

☆ **Budget Sheet** ☆

Income		
	Projected	Actual
Ticket sales @ _____ each		
Silent auction income		
Raffle income		
Sponsors		
Special donations		
Miscellaneous income		
Concessions		

Expenditures		
	Projected	Actual
Tickets		
Printed or purchased		
Space		
Rehearsal room rental		
Performance space rental		
Lighting equipment		
Sound equipment		
Sets		
Stage rental or construction		

Graphics		
	Projected	Actual
Flyers		
Posters		
Programs		
Printing, reproduction, copying		
Postage		

Legal		
	Projected	Actual
Insurance		
Royalties		
Legal fees (if applicable)		

Performance Expenses		
	Projected	Actual
Costumes		
Props		
Makeup		
Hairdressing supplies		
Vests or name tags for volunteers		
Music, CDs, tapes		
Royalties		
Miscellaneous		
Food and Drink		
Concessions		
Cast party snacks and beverages		

✫ Tally Sheet for Tracking Tickets ✫

Date _____

Show _____

Reservations

Name	Phone Number	Walk-Ins	No. of Tickets	Comps	Prepaid	Amount Received

Total tickets sold	
Total amount received	
Total monies in box office	
Minus opening cash	
Daily Total	

☆ Performer Information Sheet for Auditions ☆

You will want to modify this to reflect your own needs.

If you are producing a variety show, knowledge of daily availability for rehearsals probably won't matter, because you don't have to get the whole cast together until the dress rehearsal. However, if you are rehearsing a scripted play, which will usually require more rehearsals with the entire cast present, you may have to work around people's conflicts.

The Director's Notes section at the end of the sheet should be used by the co-directors to make notations about the audition they are watching.

Actor Information Sheet
Name: _____
Address: _____
_____

Phone: (w) _____
(h) _____
(c) _____
E-mail: _____

Auditioning for the Act: _____
Audition material: (i.e., monologue, song, act) _____
Do you sing? If so, what range? _____
Do you dance? If so, what styles? _____
Other skills?

❏ Accents
❏ Inline skating
❏ Mime
❏ Imitations
❏ Magic tricks
❏ Instruments
❏ Other _____

Scheduling Conflicts
Please list regular conflicts on the weekly calendar below. Put an "x" through times when you are NOT available for rehearsal. If the block of time already has an "x" through it, that means we will not schedule rehearsals for that time period.

Hrs.	Mon.	Tues.	Wed.	Thurs.	Fri.	Sat.	Sun.
10 A.M. - 12 P.M.	X	X	X	X	X		X
12 A.M. - 2 P.M.	X	X	X	X	X		
2 P.M. - 4 P.M.	X	X	X	X	X		
4 P.M. - 6 P.M.	X	X	X	X			
6 P.M. - 8 P.M.	X						
8 P.M. - 10 P.M.	X						

Do you have an interest in volunteering in other areas than perform-ing? If so, please check as applicable:
❏   Set construction
❏   Design
❏   Stage crew
❏   Sound
❏   Lights
❏   Costumes
❏   Makeup
❏   Hair
❏   Box office
❏   Front of House
❏   Publicity
❏   Other _____

Director's Notes:
_____
_____
_____
_____
_____
_____
_____
_____
_____
_____
_____
_____
_____
_____

☆ List of Musical Numbers ☆

Here's a chart to help you keep track of your musical needs. We've filled in the first few blanks with hypothetical acts, just to give you a sense of how to use it.

Song	Performer	Accompaniment?	Sheet Music/ Charts?	Royalties?
Welcome	Judith Little	House band	Music director to generate	N/A
Traditional bluegrass	The Country Jammers	Self-accompanied	N/A	N/A
Dancin' Cheek to Cheek	Fred and Ginger, Lucy and Rickie	CD	N/A	CHECK

⭐ **Letter to Team Leaders** ⭐

Letterhead

Name
Address

Date

Dear [Insert Name],

Thank you so much for volunteering your time and energy to make the Variety Show a huge success. [Name of community theater, organization, or group] appreciates your interest and support for [specific objective].

Please take a few minutes to fill out this evaluation form and fax or mail it to [group's fax machine and address]. This will help us plan for next year and let us know how you felt about your experience as a team leader. Your hard work and skills working with [specific area] contributed greatly to our success.

Sincerely,

_____   _____
[Co-director signature]   [Co-director signature]

_____   _____
[Co-director name]   [Co-director name]

☆ Evaluation Form for Team Leaders ☆

Name _____

Team Leader for _____

Do you feel the co-directors prepared you well for your job? What can we improve?

_____

_____

_____

_____

_____

_____

Were you kept well informed throughout the process? What can we improve?

_____

_____

_____

_____

_____

_____

Were you happy with your team members' contributions? (Y / N)

What was the best part of being a team leader for the project?

_____

_____

_____

_____

What challenges did you find in being a team leader?

_____

_____

_____

_____

What did you like best about the Variety Show?

_____

_____

_____

_____

Would you like to be a team leader again? (Y / N)

Please give any suggestions for improving the Variety Show.

_____
_____
_____
_____
_____
_____

Rules for Auctions

☆ Auction Rules ☆

Here are the rules that The Village Theatre in Issaquah, Washington, uses to set up fundraising auctions. If you want to have a similar event, you can use these as a model.

1. Upon entry, each guest will be given a bid card. To bid in the silent auction, simply write your bid number on the silent auction bid form. To bid in the live auction, hold your bid card up high with the number toward the auctioneer.
2. A bid acknowledged by the live auctioneer is a legal contract to purchase the item. In the silent auction, designation of the bid you have written by the silent auction official as the top bid is a legal contract to purchase that silent auction item.
3. Top bidders will be charged the full amount on the credit card number written on their express-pay registration card, or they can pay at the box office at the end of the event. Payment in full is mandatory at the auction.
4. Auction items will be awarded to one purchaser only. The top bid amount for an auction item will not be split among bidders who may have agreed to pay a portion of the top bid amount. Bidders who wish to split the payment for an auction item must select an individual bidder to act as purchaser. This purchaser is then responsible for full payment and for collecting the auction item(s) or certificate(s). The purchaser is also responsible for collecting individual payments from the other bidders.
5. All purchases are final and there will be no exchanges or refunds on items unless otherwise noted.

6. We will gladly accept your payment by currency, personal check, and VISA, MasterCard, or American Express. Please make your payment to Village Theatre.

7. Unless otherwise noted, all goods and services must be claimed and used within one year of the auction date.

8. Village Theatre reserves the right to add or withdraw items to or from the auction without notice.

9. Runners will collect your items for you after check out. You may be asked to show your "paid" receipt for tangible items at the door when you depart. All items must be removed from the premises the evening of the auction unless the other delivery methods are mutually agreed upon.

10. Reservations for trips and vacation accommodations must be mutually arranged with the donor unless otherwise noted. No refunds are allowed on travel packages for canceled tickets and/or accommodations.

11. Travel will be provided by donors as described, even if the prices increase above those stated. Because travel charges change, travel costs may decrease below the values stated, but no refunds will be allowed.

12. Village Theatre has attempted to describe and catalog all items correctly, but all items are offered "as is," "where is." Village Theatre neither warrants nor represents, and in no event shall be responsible for, the correctness of descriptions genuineness, authorship, provenance, or condition of items. No statement made in this catalog or made orally at the auction or elsewhere shall be deemed such as a warranty, representation, or assumption of liability. The values listed are estimates only and are not warranted for tax purposes or fair market value. Items have not been appraised unless so noted.

13. Each person issued a bid number (bidder) assumes all risks and hazards related to the auction and items obtained at the auction. Each bidder agrees to hold harmless from any liability arising there from the Village Theatre, its selected and appointed officials, members and employees, the auctioneer(s), the event organizers, sponsors, and or volunteers connected with the auction.

☆ **Silent Auction Rules** ☆

1. Items offered in the silent auction will have silent-auction bid forms attached to them or on a table nearby. You may bid by simply writing your bid number on the form opposite the amount you want to bid. The opening bid and minimum raise has been predetermined and listed on each bid sheet. We ask you to press hard, as you are making three copies.

2. You do not have to take the next amount, but may skip ahead on the form to find the amount you really want to bid. The next bidder must bid a higher amount than you did to be successful.

3. If you wish to guarantee purchase of a particular item, put your bid number next to the amount listed in the "Guaranteed Purchase Price" section of the bid sheet. Once you write your bid number on the "Guaranteed Purchase" line, the bidding on that item is concluded.

4. You may bid in any silent auction section until the section is closed. Bidding for items in the silent auction sections will close at the times posted. The silent auction official will circle the top bid number and amount. You can see if you are the successful purchaser by looking at the copy of the silent-auction bid form, which will be left after the section is closed.

☆ Live Auction Rules ☆

1. You may preview live auction items from the time the doors open until the start of the program in the auditorium. Please feel free to come right up to the display of the live items. We want you to have adequate time and opportunity to see the excellent quality of the live items. Also, please note any restrictions, limitations, sizes, etc.

2. You may bid in the live auction by holding your bid card up high with the number toward the auctioneer. Either the auctioneer or bid spotter can accept your bid.

3. The highest bidder acknowledged by the auctioneer shall be the purchaser of that live auction item. A bid acknowledged by the live auctioneer is a legal contract to purchase that item.

4. An auction volunteer will bring a bid sheet to the highest bidder acknowledged by the auctioneer. After signing the bid sheet with the bid amount, the bid sheet will be placed in your file until check out.

APPENDIX D

....

Recommended Reading

Alberts, David, *Rehearsal Management for Directors*. Portsmouth, NH: Heinemann, 1995.

Boulanger, Norman C., and Warren C. Lounsberry, *Theatre Lighting from A to Z*. Seattle and London, University of Washington Press, 1992.

Campbell, Drew, *Technical Theater for Nontechnical People*, Second Edition. New York: Allworth Press, 2004.

Cassady, Marshall, *The Book of Scenes for Acting Practice*. Lincolnwood, Ill.: National Textbook Company, 1985.

Cohen, Gary. *The Community Theater Handbook: A Complete Guide to Organizing and Running a Community Theater*. Portsmouth, NH: Heinemann Drama, 2003.

Dilker, Barbara. *Stage Management Forms and Formats: A Collection of Over 100 Forms Ready to Use*. Hollywood, CA: Quite Specific Media Group, 1991.

Hooks, Ed. *The Ultimate Scene and Monologue Sourcebook: An Actor's Guide to Over 1,000 Monologues and Scenes from 300 Contemporary Plays*. New York: Back Stage Books, 1994.

Ionazzi, Daniel A. *The Stage Management Handbook*. Cincinnati: Betterway Books, 1992.

Kaluta, John, *The Perfect Stage Crew: The Compleat Technical Guide for High School, College, and Community Theater*. New York: Allworth Press, 2004.

Kuftinec, Sonja. *Staging America: Cornerstone and Community-Based Theater*. Carbondale, IL: Southern Illinois University Press, 2005.

Spolin, Viola. *Improvisation for the Theater: A Handbook of Teaching and Directing Techniques*, Third Edition. Chicago: Northwestern University Press, 1999.

Watson, Dwight. *Original Monologues That Showcase Your Talent*. New York: Allworth Press, 2005.

Wood, David, and Janet Grant. *Theatre for Children*. Chicago: Ivan R. Dee, 1999.

Index

Books from Allworth Press

Allworth Press is an imprint of Allworth Communications, Inc. Selected titles are listed below.

Theater Festivals: Best Worldwide Venues for New Works
by Lisa Mulcahy (paperback, 6 × 9, 256 pages, $19.95)

The Health and Safety Guide for Film, TV and Theater
by Monona Rossol (paperback, 6 × 9, 256 pages, $19.95)

Technical Theater for Nontechnical People, Second Edition
by Drew Campbell (paperback, 6 × 9, 40 b&w illus., 288 pages, $19.95)

Original Monologs That Showcase Your Talent
by Dwight Watson (paperback, 5 ½ × 8 ½ 192 pages, $16.95)

Creating Your Own Monologue, Second Edition
by Glenn Alterman (paperback, 6 × 9, 256 pages, $19.95)

Acting—Advanced Techniques for the Actor, Director, and Teacher
by Terry Schreiber (paperback, 6 × 9, 256 pages, $19.95)

How to Audition for TV Commercials: From the Ad Agency Point of View
by W.L. Jenkins (paperback, 6 × 9, 208 pages, $16.95)

Improv for Actors
by Dan Diggles (paperback, 6 × 9, 246 pages, $19.95)

Movement for Actors
edited by Nicole Potter (paperback, 6 × 9, 288 pages, $19.95)

Acting for Film
by Cathy Haase (paperback, 6 × 9, 224 pages, $19.95)

Acting That Matters
by Barry Pineo (paperback, 6 × 9, 240 pages, $16.95)

Please write to request our free catalog. To order by credit card, call 1-800-491-2808 or send a check or money order to Allworth Press, 10 East 23rd Street, Suite 510, New York, NY 10010. Include $5 for shipping and handling for the first book ordered and $1 for each additional book. Ten dollars plus $1 for each additional book if ordering from Canada. New York State residents must add sales tax.

To see our complete catalog on the World Wide Web, or to order online, you can find us at
www.allworth.com.